By the same author:

Steps of Faith (Kingsway: Eastbourne, 1984). Co-authored with his wife, Judith.

Mime
The Next Step

J Geoffrey Stevenson

MINSTREL
Eastbourne

Front cover photo: Jane Morris
Illustrations by Vic Mitchell

British Library Cataloguing in Publication Data

Stevenson, Geoffrey, *1951–*
Mime: The Next Step
1. Mime
I. Title
792.3

ISBN 1–85424–032–3

Printed in Great Britain for
Minstrel, an imprint of Monarch Publications Ltd,
1 St Anne's Road, Eastbourne, East Sussex BN21 3UN by
Courier International Ltd, Tiptree, Essex
Typeset by J&L Composition Ltd, Filey, North Yorkshire

Contents

Acknowledgements	7
Foreword	8
Preface	10
PART 1: The Basics	15
1. Running The Workshop	17
2. Workshop Ingredients	24
3. Work-out!	31
4. Resources – I	36
5. Resources – II	46
PART 2: The Workshops	51
6. Workshop Summaries	53
7. Workshop 1	56
8. Workshop 2	62
9. Workshop 3	69
10. Workshop 4	76
11. Workshop 5	81
12. Workshop 6	85
13. Workshop 7	89
14. Workshop 8	96
15. Workshop 9	100
16. Workshop 10	106
PART 3: The Sketches	109
17. The Chocolate Box	112
18. Deck-chairs on the Titanic	117
19. Dreaming	124
20. The Good News Is Like . . .	130
21. The History of Music	135
22. The Addicts	143

23. Kitchen Sink	151
24. Unemployment	155
25. Behold Your God	162
26. The Heavenly City	166
27. Mime to Songs	170
Glossary	175
Appendix 1: Mime Theatre	177
Appendix 2: Mime in Public and Private Worship	181
Bibliography	187

Acknowledgements

My thanks must go first to my wife, Judith, for bringing out the best in me and putting up with the rest; to Paul Burbridge, for the Foreword, and David Smith for the word in season; to Shirley Horsman for her patience, and fast, accurate typing; to Sandra Goodwill and the Drama Group of St Michael-le-Belfry Church, York, for always wanting to take the next step; and lastly, eternally, to my Lord Jesus . . . but words fail me.

Foreword

A quick glance through the contents of this book might perplex the casual browser through the average religious bookstall. Selections such as 'Advanced Hand Exercises' are not normally encountered, except perhaps in some avant garde tome about prayer. 'Face Exercises' present an even greater challenge to the spiritually minded, as does the idea of beginning a small-group meeting with a round of silly games. Are we in another world? In a sense the answer is yes. In this immensely practical and readable book, Geoffrey Stevenson opens a door into a world where silence is rivetting, and where precise visual communication creates a universal language which entertains, moves, instructs and lingers in the mind long after the words have subsided. He does so as an accomplished artist, carefully unveiling the secrets of his craft, and as a committed Christian whose faith has provided the inspiration to work and perform for the glory of his Creator.

This is not merely a book for mime specialists. While the approach is thoroughly professional, the teaching given shows great sensitivity to the limitations of the amateur performer and the needs of the local church theatre group. Those who simply want to explore mime without the pressure of doing it in front of other people will find much to encourage them here. The word 'fun' is often used, though a certain amount of muscular pain seems unavoidable if the excellent ready-made workshops are to be taken seriously. There is even food for thought in this book for preachers, leaders of small groups and those who through a physical interpretation of Scripture will understand aspects of truth which they never perceived before. There is no doubt that, if explored creatively, the contents of this book would enrich the worship and communication of any church. There are many people, I know, who will be itching to get their hands on the various mime scripts, some of which are the classics of the Geoffrey Stevenson repertoire.

The simple visual aid, the telling gesture, has always increased the effectiveness of the most memorable communicators: without the power of *the action*, Jesus would never have so impressed upon his disciples the need to wash one another's feet as an expression of humility and love – apart from Peter's outburst, the silence of concentration that filled the Upper Room must have been profound. To rediscover the art of mime, as Geoffrey explains, is to rediscover something of the imagination of the biblical prophets, whose *demonstration* of God's word was occasionally the most unforgettable aspect of their preaching. Mime is a gentle art, but the vulnerability of the silent performer, as I have often seen, is rewarded by a level of attention and involvement from the audience which few other art forms ever achieve; it is hard to walk away from a silence which is so filled with delight, mystery and intrigue. Skilful mime commands respect since its tone can never hector or bully. It is a 'still small voice' which the church so often needs.

If ever there was a book which called for *action*, this is it.

PAUL BURBRIDGE

Preface

'Mime is dead'.

Those were the words, when I met him recently, of Richmond Shepard, author of the book on mime that gave me a start fourteen years ago. In some ways I agree with him. While preparing for this book I had a good look at what has already been written on the subject, most of it published in America.

It was a little depressing. Like studying Latin, really. Very beautiful and fascinating, but a dead language. Nobody speaks it anymore. That's why all the books are so old and, by and large, out of print.

So much mime these days is either broad slapstick, for which the highest praise is 'inventive', or technical virtuosity, which may impress but can never move. Jacques Lecoq is the modern master of an approach to mime that tries to go beyond the 'Marcell Marceau' school of illusionary pantomime. He pointed out:

> During the Roman era, one mimed philosophical discourses; and one day the great mime Roscius mimed a discourse of Cicero with his feet; this marked the end of pantomime, which was killed by its own virtuosity.

To put it another way, why should one be interested in actions – lifting an imaginary weight, leaning on an invisible wall – that one would not bother to watch in real life? I believe, however, that at the heart of these criticisms lies an acknowledgement of the emptiness at the heart of much contemporary art. On the whole it does not have anything to say, and so innovation becomes the primary aim.

In these days of glossy sophisticated entertainment – ten channels beamed straight into the living room – is there any place for a simple low-tech art form like mime? And simple it must be. Whereas it may be accompanied by colour and music and, yes, noises made by the performers themselves – it remains an art form whose virtue is created by a 'doing without'. It is *poor* theatre, theatre at its simplest: an audience, a space and an actor with a story to tell.

Mime is rather like sharing the gospel – it works best when we are weakest. Take away words and language, and the body speaks – often profoundly – of the soul's state. In simplicity and poverty there is spiritual authenticity and integrity. Or there can be. It depends, too, on a receptive audience.

One of the great privileges of my work has been to use mime to communicate across enormous divides of culture, class and age. Old people in Gothenburg, Sweden and Greenwich, Connecticut; teenagers in Soweto and Utrecht; stroke patients in York, and students in New York.

Adults and children from a poor fishing village in the Philippines have laughed in the right places, but it puzzles me more when well-to-do American kids do as well. I know that a lot of Western European teenagers, seduced by the media, are too 'sophisticated' for mime. Perhaps the Americans have had so much fancy entertainment all their lives that they are struck by the simplicity and immediacy of the art form.

This book is a sequel to my first one, *Steps of Faith*, which was an introduction to mime in the church. Five years on I still believe that mime has tremendous potential to speak to hearts and minds, contribute to worship and communicate spiritual truth to our culture. It has in fact a dual potential to tell of God: explicitly, in its stories and themes, and implicity – as human creativity, when redeemed, reflects the glory of the Creator–Redeemer of mankind.

In this book I am attempting to provide basic training for an individual or a group who are prepared to follow instructions, be imaginative and work hard. Like any art form, mime has certain basic techniques that must be mastered before anything can be expressed. I am therefore writing primarily for young adults who are interested in exploring and experimenting in one of the dramatic arts. I am also writing for the not-so-young who are prepared to get fit. By the way, thirty is a great age to start, according to Desmond Jones, London's foremost teacher of mime.

At the centre of this book is a series of ten workshops intended to introduce a group to the hard work and the fun of mime.

Hard work, because the mastery of mime techniques does not come easily. The aim is to make it *look* easy, of course, but just like beginning a musical instrument, there is much tedious practising of scales before a tune may be played.

Fun, because mime is a kind of *play-acting* and there is a child in all of us who loves to play-act, given a safe enough environment.

These workshops are for any number from four up to twelve or fifteen, and are intended to be held on a regular weekly basis. Over the ten weeks, a simple discipline of movement will be established and a range of mime techniques taught in the context of a dance and drama group who are prepared to give themselves to the study of mime.

Before the workshops are some explanatory notes on the kind of leadership required and what to expect from a group. Chapter two looks at the theory behind some of the elements of the workshops. Chapter three introduces the work-out or limbering up that you need to do at the beginning of a workshop and Chapters four and five are a resource section, with detailed explanation of different exercises used in the series. In Chapter six a summary of the ingredients is given, followed by detailed sections covering each new technique or game as it is needed. The workshops could be designed to a similar pattern which is usually: loosening up, technique-work and improvisation.

The book also contains an outline of ten mime pieces, along with guidelines for creating mime to songs. Some of these are solo, some are for group mime of up to four persons. There is a glossary of the technical terms and abbreviations used in this book, and the appendices consist of two essays, one on mime theatre technique and one on mime in public and private worship, which you will need to read as preparation for two of the later workshops.

Returning to my opening remark, no, I do not think mime is dead. But if you master the art of mime – and it will take a lot more than this book to help you – don't expect to be in great demand on the working men's club circuit, a star-turn at the Royal Variety Command Performance or the recipient of £25,000 from the Arts Council. Expect instead to reach people in simple ways and in simple situations. Give them your heart, and pray that it beats with the heartbeat of God.

PART 1

The Basics

I
Running The Workshop

A group may be able to follow the workshop outline closely, but it is much better if there is a leader who is especially familiar with the material. You need not be vastly experienced in mime, but you do need to have studied and practised as far as possible each week's material in advance of the rest of the class. Naturally, you also need to have the confidence of the group if you are going to lead with authority. And two of the qualities needed to gain that respect are *competence* and *servanthood*.

Competence for this kind of thing is perhaps not easily assessed in advance, but the leader should at least be able to plan and carry out the forming of a group in the church. This means clearing it with the church leadership, and explaining the vision, aims and goals. It means booking a room to work in, making sure it's warm and that access (the key) is taken care of *before* turning up with only one minute to go before class. It means spreading the word about the class, and looking out for those in the church who might have a talent. It means gauging the likely interest so as not to be the only one who does turn up!

When – if – the group comes to performing, a cool head, an ability to think ahead, and a mania for details are necessary. These will certainly help you if you find that, for example, with nine minutes to go before the evening service, the person in charge of the sound doesn't have the type of leads you need to plug your cassette deck into the church sound system. All your vital and beautifully recorded sound cues are in danger, along with the sketch, your contribution to the service and the church's first opportunity to see what the mime group have been doing over there in the hall all these weeks.

After uttering a prayer along the lines of 'Dear God ... help!' you search through your bag and, with an exultant cry that confirms the church warden's fears about the excesses of charismaniacs, you find that out of the several leads you threw in at home 'just in case', there is one that will do the job.

There is a moral to this tale, which as it happens is very fresh in my own memory, and it is: 'Expect the best, and always prepare for the worst.'

But equally necessary – in fact a higher quality – is the attitude of *a servant*. Naturally you want your own skills in mime to improve, but the group needs a leader who is there to serve and to enable others to grow.

Remember that when you can't find anyone who will take responsibility for washing up the coffee cups afterwards;

When the shyest girl in the group tearfully tells you that you aren't being fair in giving out parts to play;

When the church leadership forgets to thank you for the sketch last Sunday, remember what Jesus said as he washed his disciples' feet.

Having said all that, the church is not served by having leaders who are treated as doormats, but teaching to correct that is beyond the scope of this book.

Being able to pray and worship together is, of course, vital to a group that aspires to ministry. You will need to worship in a way with which everyone is most comfortable, but be careful not to sink to a lowest common denominator out of fear of one another. The leader needs to know something about informal worship, extemporaneous prayer and small group dynamics.

Still feel you want to lead a group? Read on, it gets better.

'OK, everybody, let's make a start'

The qualities to look for in the group are: promptness, commitment, a willingness to grow in trust and openness with one another, a desire to work hard physically and mentally and a degree of maturity that will take criticism and frank comments.

Promptness – it's only once a week, and for the sake of group unity, as well as the vital warming-up period, class members should arrive in good time to take off outer clothing, change shoes, say their hellos, and settle down. Members should be strongly encouraged to be on time for the limbering-up and stretching. This is necessary before any strenuous work – it helps people to avoid injury, and is also the way to complete physical and mental participation in the rest of the class.

Commitment is important. Very, *very* important. After two or three sessions, people should either go, or be prepared to stay with the group for at least three months. It is a good idea to talk this through with everyone at the outset of working together. This need not be a 'heavy' session, or legalistic in outlook. Rather, it should be possible for everyone to agree on how desirable it is to be committed. This is far better for the unity and identity of the group. It is also good for us as individuals, since we all benefit at times from being forced through psychological barriers, instead of giving up the moment our enthusiasm temporarily drops off.

Expect relationships to grow during the course of time that a drama or mime group is together. Trusting and open relationships are often the result of working closely together, especially when you are vulnerable through being exposed to one another. But such relationships are also the *condition* for working effectively together. This is true in a theatrical sense as well as a spiritual one.

As anyone knows, growing closer means learning to love – and love hurts. We will need to practise forgiveness and the deliberate setting aside of bitterness and resentment. Some of us will find jealousy or envy a temptation. Others will fall into insensitive independence. We will all be inclined at some point to think that certain patterns of behaviour, usually, in 'the others', will never change for the better. These things will have to be worked through and may need pastoral oversight.

Competition (except in the case of certain games) should be discouraged. As for taking criticism, well – one of the most difficult areas of theatre is the performer's ego. You'd think it would be easier among Christians. After all, they should be crucifying their sins of pride, preferring others to themselves, laying down their lives for their brethren and so on. But as we all know, it doesn't seem to work like that. If anything, the director or leader feels even more anxiety than his counterpart in 'the world', lest anyone within the body of Christ be needlessly hurt by unkind remarks. It is the same in many areas of church life where gifts and ministries are being actively exercised. People are deeply involved, and rightly so, in their work for the Lord, but so many of us also come to depend on that work for our sense of importance and self-worth. The problem is not confined to drama and mime, but it is acute in those areas because we are involved, you might say, with the very tools of the job: our body and our personality.

Again and again we need to strike a balance between high standards and people's feelings. For instance, there may be someone who really wants to stay in the group but who has absolutely no talent, and can't see and won't accept that fact. The whole situation is very difficult. Naturally, you don't wish to hurt him or her, and you know that negative remarks are bound to cause hurt and deep discouragement, possibly ruining the good atmosphere of the rehearsal or workshop. As soon as this person also begins to show signs of clinging on to a patently false hope of ever being good, it is probably going to be necessary to steer them away from performing. Such a problem or blind spot will be a source of pain to themselves and a continual hindrance to the group. The leader has a particular need to be full of grace and truth, and it is a great gift to be able to point out faults in a way that does not discourage.

Of course, a person should not be excluded simply because he or she is *bad*. There will, I hope, be those with a refreshing maturity who desire to explore mime as a hobby, even though they'll never be good at it. They don't wish to put themselves forward, have no need of performing in public, and are not clinging on to what they feel is *their* ministry or calling. Do not discourage such people. The arts are for ordinary folks, too, so that something of God's creativity and sense of fun and play may be enjoyed. For more on this aspect of the arts as play, see *Steps of Faith*, pp 27–29, and also *The Folk Arts in Renewal* by Patricia Beal and Martha Keys Barker (Hodder & Stoughton: London, 1980).

The group must be submitted to the leadership of the church, but it also needs to feel that the church leadership is behind it and understands the vision for this kind of work. Is it too much to expect an occasional visit from the leader or elder to whose sermons they might be enriching or adding something?

The mechanics of working together in a church group of this kind are complex. You may find many of my wife's remarks helpful in this area (see the chapter on 'The Dance Group' in her half of *Steps of Faith*. You may, however, disregard paragraphs such as, 'What to wear for the evening service.')

That brings me to a few practical points, such as what to wear for the workshop. Look for form-fitting clothing that allows for free movement, such as exercise pants, track-suit, stretch jeans (but not ordinary jeans) and a T-shirt or close-fitting sweatshirt, or a leotard for women. The clothing should not be too baggy – after all, people need to see what you are doing.

What you wear on your feet is important. The sole of the shoe must be thin and flexible to allow the foot to bend freely. Soft canvas or leather acrobatic shoes are ideal. Trainers are out, so are new ballet shoes – the sole is too stiff. Old ballet shoes may be all right, or just socks. Bare feet won't slide well. Best of all, although it is an investment, are leather *Jazz shoes* with suede or rubber soles. You can get them from Freed's or Gamba (dancewear shops) in London. They cost around £20 at the time of writing.

The optimum time for the class will of course depend on who's coming. A weekday evening may suit single people with busy weekends. Saturdays may suit teenagers with homework to do during the week and parents with young children who can be left with the spouse. Warn people that those involved in a particular sketch for a Sunday service or outreach, will need to be able to give extra rehearsal time. Lots of extra rehearsal time.

The optimum length for a class is probably an hour and three quarters for a small number. It may take longer if the class numbers ten or more. Note that this does not include time for chatting, fellowshipping and coffee afterwards.

Try to find a regular place to meet that is warm, spacious and clean enough to sit and lie on the floor happily. In my experience, the ideal is about fifty square feet of floor space per person, completely free of furniture. Enough chairs for everyone to have a seat would be an advantage, but not a necessity. In cold weather arrange for heating to come on before the workshop starts; it can be dangerous to do workouts or warm-ups in a cold room.

Finally, where a technique has been covered in *Steps of Faith*, it will be necessary to refer to a copy of that for a fuller explanation. This happens frequently, so keep it handy.

2
Workshop Ingredients

Games

At several points in the workshop series I will suggest and describe certain games. These should not be seen as a childish diversion, beneath the serious actor's attention. (Anyone with that solemn an attitude to himself and to theatre needs watching.) Nor should they be skipped over as not worth the time. They can be immensely valuable to the work of a mime group, in several ways.

One of the most significant is the removal of fear. Many people – not just Christians – bring to acting and mime a fear of failing, of exposing themselves, of appearing a fool. Games allow us to participate, to expose ourselves, and to 'fail' or make mistakes in a non-threatening and secure situation. We are not in competition with each other – we are together attempting to overcome an obstacle or solve a problem. Group activities (particularly fun ones) give security and anonymity – particularly important to shyer members.

In fact, enjoyment such as is generated by good games is vital to group identity. I would say it is about as important as praying together – certainly it is an ingredient in the kind of open, honest, relaxed and trusting relationships there should be in the body of Christ.

Games encourage the flow of communication and the sensitivity to one another necessary for good dramatic work together. The role-playing in many games is of course a very helpful preparation for acting, while allowing people freedom to express themselves and develop their own ideas.

Physical contact is another great Anglo-Saxon fear. We do not have a great many social conventions that permit us to touch one another, and we are only conforming to our cultural and racial stereotype when we say we prefer it that way. Games provide a safe environment to break down that barrier of fear, paving the way to greater freedom on stage and the ability to demonstrate relationships there in physically appropriate and truthful ways.

Some extremely good books have been written on games and acting exercises: (see the bibliography). Two that I am drawing on for this book are: *Acting: A Drama Studio Source Book* by John Miles Brown (Peter Owen: London), and *The Gamesters' Handbook* by Donna Brandes and Howard Phillips (Century Hutchinson: London) – 140 games for teachers and group leaders.

Homework

Homework is an important aspect of the workshop programme, for several reasons. First, it encourages students to work outside class time. If they are going to grow, they must practise during the week as a matter of course, not only on homework but also on the techniques. Secondly, it gives students who are particularly prone to improvisational paralysis – of the rabbit-caught-in-the-headlights-of-an-oncoming-car variety – the chance to work on something at their own pace. Thirdly, it's great for saving class-time.

The first homework assignments are very simple, primarily to ensure that techniques learnt in class are practised during the week. The experience of showing something all by oneself to the rest of the group builds confidence and prepares for more adventurous performances later on.

Suggest that people spend half an hour or so on 'assignments', and encourage them not to leave it until just before the class! Be sure that showing the homework doesn't get squeezed out during class. At least have everyone show quickly what they have done, even if there isn't time for critique. If the assignment has been for something major, it is often a good idea to go over the homework fairly early in the class, after warming up and playing a game together, so that any anxiety individuals may have about what they have to do does not distract them from other work. If there seems to be enough time, by all means allow everyone a few minutes to refresh their memory before showing what they have done.

Be sure to give out the assignment for the following week very clearly at the end of the class, complete with threats, dire warnings of penalties for failure to produce, etc.

Improvisation

By this I mean anything created in class-time without a great deal of rehearsal, preparation and planning. True improvisation (push 'em out on stage and let's see what happens) is extremely difficult, unless you are very talented, very quick and quite experienced at it. In that case it's only fairly difficult.

In the workshops, however, we will be making it easier by allowing preparation times. There is still a release of adrenalin when that time is short, but the aim is to recognise and appreciate it, harness it and use it to fire the performance.

Quite often, too, the inspiration that occurs bears no relation to the amount of time afforded it. Wonderful ideas can spring up which delight and encourage everyone. Of course performers are limited to techniques they are already familiar with, and there is no time for complicated routines to be worked out, nor for sophisticated plot or split-second timing. A lack of understanding of basic stage-craft may well cripple an idea, but that in turn is the best time to correct such faults.

Egos are less on the line with quickly produced performances and criticism should be easier to give. There is always the let-out (for instructor and student): 'Of course there was so little time.'

The general progression therefore should be from giving just two to three minutes' preparation time in early improvisations to allowing up to twenty minutes of class-time for devising and rehearsing. Give the title or theme of the exercise, explain what it means, with the outline of an example, state how long it is to be or rather, how short, (and what will happen to them if they run over), and how much time they are going to be allowed to work on it. Split them into the right-sized groups if it is not a solo exercise, and tell them to find a space and start working.

Emphasise the need for *simplicity* and make sure they don't spend more than 20% of the time talking and thinking about it. They should settle on an idea quickly, however simple it seems, and then stand up and start working it out.

When time is up, bring them back and have them perform what they have done. Create an audience area and a performing area which is the 'stage', indicate where the 'wings' are (where those who are off are really off) and how far forward performers can come. Ask for respectful silence from the rest of the class, and make sure that each offering begins and ends with several counts of pure stillness. Many is the time a perfectly acceptable ending has been ruined by underconfident performers rushing to get off before the audience knows that the piece is even finished.

If you think of it, you might diplomatically ensure that those who are likely to do the best work are last, or at least not first, lest they discourage everyone else. (There is more on critiques and the process of assessment later.)

In the early stages of rehearsing a piece, before it has been cast, short scenes can be the subject of *semi-improvised* work. Give each small group – or solo performers – the same piece to work on by themselves, interpreting the script as best they can. It may be only twenty seconds of closely worked-out business. Consider using some members of the class as directors, if they would prefer it and seem to have an aptitude. After fifteen minutes, bring them together and have them perform each little snippet of the sketch, putting the segment in context of the whole sketch if necessary, for the enjoyment and understanding of those watching.

This method is very valuable when rehearsing or creating a sketch. Use it to note different character interpretations that emerge, some of which you will want to keep, and some of which may alter your whole perception of the piece. It is also of course a very useful method of 'auditioning' the members of the group for casting in the piece, if that has not been done.

Critiques

Allow time when viewing work for constructive criticism and assessment. You can do it immediately after each performance, while memories are fresh, or you can wait until all have performed, when egos are a little less tender. The latter option allows people to make comparative evaluations that are not that helpful, so I prefer making the critique following each piece.

When criticizing point out what is working and what is good, as well as faults. Invite, if there is time, comments from the rest of the group. It should go without saying that all criticisms must come from a generous, open spirit. They should also be expressed sensitively, in a way that the individual receiving them can accept.

There will be times when some will have performed markedly more successfully than the rest. While not withholding praise for their work, it is a good moment to make the point to the others that failure is the breeding ground for improvement (the only thing we learn from success is what we're really good at!). This is not to drag down someone if they have done well, but to revive and restore crushed and flagging spirits.

The following are helpful questions you can ask the rest of the class (or yourself as director):

1. What did you like about it? (Start with the positive.)
2. What parts worked? What made you laugh (if that was the aim), or moved or affected you?
3. What was done well?
4. Ask the performer(s) what parts worried them.
5. What wasn't clear? Why not?
6. Was there a good use of space – could everything be seen properly?
7. Was the focus of attention clear?
8. Was the piece economical in its use of movements?
9. Did it have a good moment of silence at the beginning and end?
10. Did the piece have a good beginning and a definite conclusion?
11. Was there *rhythmical variety* in the piece – ie fast/slow?
12. Did it have energy, vitality, freshness?
13. Did the performers have energy, vitality, freshness?
14. Did they take command of the stage?
15. Were the characters developed – or on their way?

The most important question to ask, in some way or another, is:

16. Could everybody understand what was going on?

Performed mime should not be a game of charades, with prizes to those members of the audience who can guess what's going on.

End with praise for something and a suggestion of an area to work on. Be specific. Don't be like the director who told his cast after the first night, 'I have only one "note" for you: act better!'

3
Work-out!

In every workshop, in fact each time you practice or perform mime, you should begin by warming up. How much of a work-out you do at the beginning of the workshops really depends on how serious you want to be.

For the church group, meeting by and large once a week, a limber-up rather than a full work-out, is perhaps more relevant. A period of ten or fifteen minutes loosens the joints, stretches the muscles, relieves some of the stress accumulated during the day, gets the blood circulating, wakes up the brain and reduces the chance of injury later on.

A really good *work-out*, on the other hand, should be an introduction to and a development of the different kinds of movement needed for mime technique. At its best it develops strength, flexibility, control and stamina. In this case we are talking discipline and hard work, *punishing* the body to get it into shape, several times a week, week after week.

This may be just one person's goal. There are not many who have the motivation to work this hard, but it is the only way to excel in a professional sphere.

For the more modest purposes of this book, there are three levels of limbering up. If you are following the workshops with a group, you will need to settle on one and stick to it, at least for a time. Details will be found in the *Resource* section,

Chapters 4 and 5, where you will also find other exercises used from time to time in the workshops.

A. For 5–10 minutes of simple stretch and limber, try the following.

Everyone lies on the floor, and does 'The Cat'.

Stand, and then shake out every part of the body, starting with the fingers, and progressing until every part of the body is in motion.

Finish off with a good running game such as 'tag'. This is for the sake of both the *aerobic* or cardiovascular (ie how well the heart and lungs pump oxygen around the body) benefit, and the group interaction and unity.

B. For an intermediate kind of warm-up, lasting 14 minutes, do the one outlined in the 'Make It Work' section of *Steps of Faith*.

It is quite simple, it stretches and strengthens most muscle groups appropriate to mime, and it introduces some of the isolations studied in mime technique.

This work-out is also available accompanied by music on the cassette *Music for Mime* by Christopher Norton and Geoffrey Stevenson, published by Ears and Eyes Music. It is available by post from: Anfield Distribution, 276 Monument Road, Edgbaston, Birmingham B16 8XF, or any good Christian bookshop.

C. For a more advanced work-out, lasting up to 45 minutes, you will want to make your own, gleaning what you can from mime courses, modern dance and ballet classes, acrobatic, tumbling and clowning workshops, gymnastics, etc. People have even been known to do Jane Fonda's Workout. (But be sensible and don't 'go for the burn' at the wrong time and before you understand what you're doing.)

Before doing any of the above work-outs, however, I recommend the following procedure to relax the body, give it a chance to melt away some of the tensions which can lead to injuries, and *warn* it of what is to come.

Lie on your back, arms relaxed at your sides, at a 45° angle.

Draw your feet in and knees up, feeling the contact with the floor of the whole of your spine. Press the small of your back towards the floor, drawing your knees further towards your chin if necessary to feel the floor. Lengthen the back of the neck, to close the gap between your neck and the floor, by pulling your chin toward your chest.

Let the feet slide away and the legs stretch out, all the while trying to maintain floor contact with the whole of your spine. Then go through a sequence of wriggling each part of the body separately: first the fingers, then the whole hand, then the wrist, etc. until you have moved every part of the body at least once.

This sequence is described in greater detail at the beginning of 'Make It Work' in *Steps of Faith*, p 88.

I may as well be honest with you. Working as hard as all this on your own is not easy. If you run or jog regularly, and particularly if you have trained for and run in a Marathon, you'll know what I mean. It can be done. I will not attempt any amateur psychology to explain how to do it, as it depends on the personality. But whatever level you stick at, I would urge you take very seriously this aspect of the work.

Several times in my career, as I contemplated a course of secular training (or even just a work-out on a Monday morning), I have asked the Lord, 'Is this necessary?' and 'Is this spiritual?' Sometimes it seems so worldly, possibly leading to introverted or narcissistic concern for self. And each time the Lord has in effect told me to go deeper, to master my craft, to get my hands dirty in the stuff, the conflicts and the mysteries of living down here, instead of performing with my head in a super-spiritual cloud.

Of course we all know about the very real dangers of doing Christian work 'in our own strength'. We need discernment, watchfulness and, perhaps most of all, friends and ministers who will be honest with us. But the opposite danger is just as damaging to the work of extending the kingdom of God: complacency. This is often brought on by a lack of confidence in God's calling, an attitude which says, 'I'm just dabbling in this, I'll never be any good'.

What is really funny – or sad – is when the same people who appear to have that attitude are completely devastated when it is suggested to them that in truth they are not any good, and perhaps their gifts lie elsewhere.

The question of whether you have a calling or gift from the Lord needs to be approached with common sense as much as anything else. Mime is a craft, like acting, pottery, or computer programming. To be any good, you have to have some talent, some enthusiasm, and a willingness to work at it.

Whether that talent can be used by the Lord depends on other character traits and attributes, such as: humility, 'teachability', sensitivity to congregational worship, and a creative imagination that can be reined in as well as gallop freely.

Are you searching for a sense of God's calling in your use of such a gift? Try to seek as much advice, direction and criticism from those you respect as possible, while working very, very hard all the time at holding your desires on an 'open palm', as it were, before God. Don't make it hard for others to tell you painful truths, or you will never hear the truth. And, of course pray and read the Scriptures. Keep on asking; He will answer.

Whatever the size of our gifts, we need to remember the parable of the talents, and neither despise nor be stupidly fearful regarding the gifts and potential abilities the Lord has given us. Preparation without prayer is pride. Prayer without preparation is presumption. Hard work to the limit of our abilities, and soaked in prayer, is the path to seeing God at work.

4
Resources – I

Stretch and Limber-up: 'The Cat'

Begin on the foor, lying on your side, curled up as tightly as possible.

Close your eyes, and imagine you are turned completely in on yourself. Draw into yourself everything about you – your arms, hands, legs, feet, your energy, your spirit (rather like some cats I know).

Now begin to stretch, as if you are a cat waking up.

Reach out with one arm, and stretch – a big long stretch.

Do the same with the leg on the same side.

Stretch arm and leg together, from toes to fingertips.

Roll over and repeat on the other side.

On your hands and knees, curve and pull your back up as high as you can, tucking your chin into your chest, and pulling the pelvis under.

Then reverse it, slowly, gently, but going to the limit, make the spine bend the other way as you stretch your chin to the ceiling.

Stretch one leg behind as far as possible.

Now the other one.

Still on your knees, sit back onto your heels, and bend down until your chest is on your thighs, and your chin on your knees. (More or less!)

Reach your hands out in front as far as they will go and place your palms on the ground. This is the starting position for the next series of moves.

Lift your bottom and begin to come up, but keep your chin as close to the ground as you can, while moving your head towards your hands.

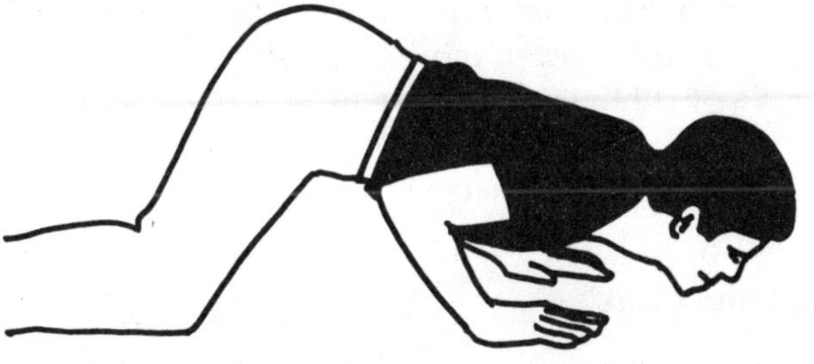

'The Cat'

With your weight on your hands, stretch forward with your chin leading until your body is straight. Then continue the movement, arching your back, straightening your arms, and pushing your chin to the ceiling.

'The Cat'

Hold it there for a few seconds.

Now return to the first position, lifting your bottom first, arching your back, sitting back on your heels and folding yourself down again, with your hands still stretched in front.

Begin the forward movement again as before, until your back is arched and your chin is raised, then immediately begin the return movement. When you get back down again, go straight into the forward movement until the whole sequence is a cycle of continuous movement.

Repeat seven times. Slowly sit up, then stand. (Speed may be increased in later sessions).

Basic Hand Exercises

Flexibility, strength and control in the hands are of immense importance to mime of all kinds, but particularly illusory mime and the handling of imaginary objects.

1. Stretch the hands out to the side at shoulder height (might as well strengthen the arms while we're at it) and open and close them really hard eight times.

2. Then open and close the fingers, bending at the middle knuckle, eight times.

3. Put the hands in front of you, palms up, waist high, elbows bent, and make the hand flat and very rigid. Reach the thumb of each hand across the palm, as far as it will go, and back again, always keeping the rest of the hand flat. Do this eight times.

4. Clench the fist tightly, then sharply throw open and spread the fingers as wide as possible in front of you, palms facing the body. Do this eight times.

5. Turn the palms away from you, and throw the palms, as it were, about four inches onto an imaginary wall. Make the hand as flat as possible, and come to a complete stop, with *the sharpest* movement possible (against the 'wall') each time before relaxing the hands and forearms as you bring them away. Do this eight times.

'Throw the palms on to a "wall"' (5)

'Curl the fingers in' (6)

6. Hold the hands at the level of your face, palms facing away, and curl the fingers in, one by one, thumb first, then index finger, etc., keeping the remaining ones as straight as possible for as long as possible. Turn palms towards the body and uncurl them, strictly one by one. Do this four times.
7. Then for eight seconds wriggle all the fingers together quite fast in front of you, in as many different ways as possible, not forgetting the thumbs.
8. Finally, put one hand palm up in front of you, take hold of the fingers with the other hand (fingers on top, thumb underneath) and bend the fingers down as far as they will go. You are bending back the wrist at the same time – let that happen. Be sure the arm is straight. After eight slowish tugs or yanks, give sixteen more sharp pulls down on the same hand and wrist. Then switch and do the same on the other

hand (and wrist). This is an important preparation for advanced work with the hands . . .

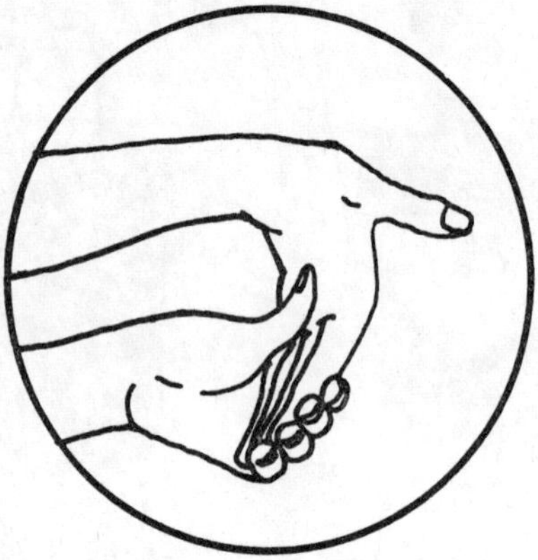

'Bend the fingers down as far as they will go.' (8)

Wrist Exercises

Hold the hands up in front of your face, in line with the forearms, palms facing each other. Fingers together, keeping them parallel, flat and rigid, bend them sideways at the wrist.

'Bend them sideways at the wrist'

Then move them across twelve inches in the opposite direction. Stop. Snap them over so they are bent in the other direction. Move them together – they must stay parallel – across in front of you. At the other end of their travel, snap them over as before, and move them across again. The effect should be a motion that appears to be led by the wrists.

Now do the same thing but with the palms facing away from you: the hands tilt to one side while moving the other way, with the wrist-bone leading. At the end of their travel the hands flip over and move back.

Advanced Hand Exercises

1. Place palms together, fingers together and up as if in prayer, cross the thumbs, and then force the hands straight down. Push them down, keeping every part of the two palms glued together as long as possible (stretch the wrists). As the heels of the palms separate, let the fingers lace through each other and continue to push down until

2a

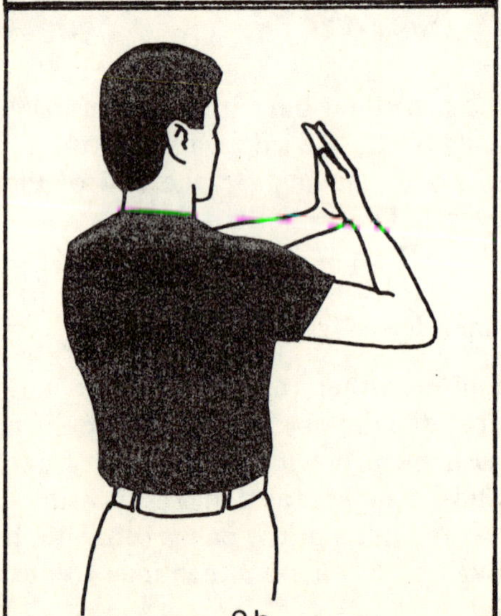

2b

the hands separate completely. (Lots of knuckles will 'crack' here – I don't think that does any harm, but if you don't like it, don't do it.) Repeat three times.

2a. Place hands together in front of your face, fingers together and use the pressure from the fingers of one hand to force the fingers of the other hand back in a smooth curve, as far as they will go. Alternate hands, four times.

2b. Same position, same pressure, but this time keep the fingertips and the bases of palms where they are, and just press out the middle of the hands. Do this four times.

Appreciate these two different movements and the control required.

3a. The Spider

Spread the fingers of one hand wide and then force palm (the middle of the hand) out, trying for a reverse curvature of the hand similar to that achieved in the last exercise. Holding that curve of the hand, curl/bend the tips of the fingers forwards, so that the hand, when viewed from the side, makes an S curve. Then relax. Repeat several times with each hand. Do the same thing with fingers together.

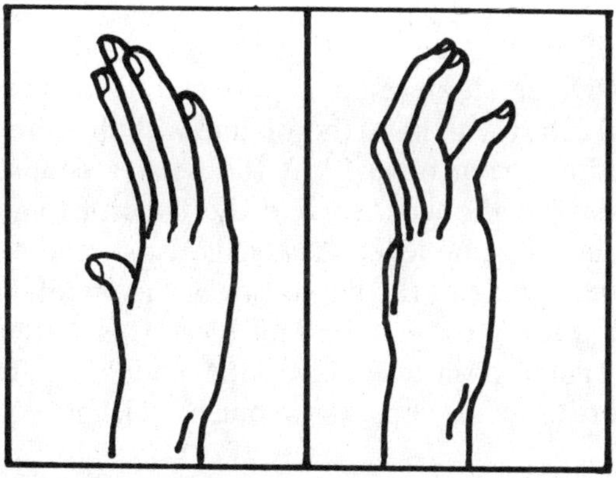

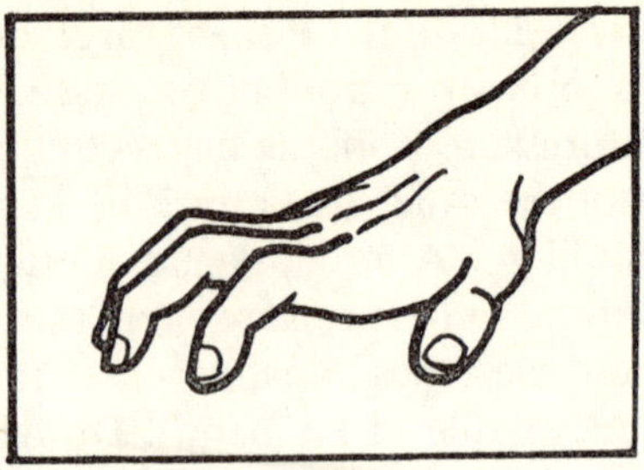

3b. I call it 'The Spider' because you can practise it on a table top. Placing your hand flat on the table, lift the fingers off the table while the centre of the palm stays down. When they are as high as you can make them, bring the fingertips down to touch the table, leaving the middle knuckles up in the air where they are. (Somewhat spider-like, no?) Straighten the fingers so they are curved up again, then lower them down to the table top. Repeat several times to each hand.

The S shape is known in *Decroux* mime technique as *La Salamandre*. The flat hand is called *La Planche*. The curved hand is called *La Coquille*. Now you know.

4. Undulations

Finally, create/develop an undulating movement in the hand. Start with hand flat, in line with the forearm, fingers together, palm down. Lift the wrist a couple of inches, bending at the wrist so that the fingertips and the elbow stay at the same level. Lower the wrist, and as you do so, lift the middle of the hand. Lower the middle of the hand, while raising the middle knuckles. This will pass through the spider position. Lower the middle knuckles as the fingertips come up. It is much quicker doing it than explaining it. The effect, when smooth, is a wave motion which passes through the hand.

You should practise this until it is very smooth and can be varied in size, from a wave involving the whole arm, beginning at the shoulder, to a tiny ripple that passes through the fingertips. Practise this ripple or undulation of the hand until you can do it with the absolute minimum of vertical movement – as if your hand is sandwiched between two parallel boards two inches apart.

This undulation is important to master, because it is terrifically useful for conveying many kinds of movement found in nature such as wind and waves. It is certainly not just for body-popping, which is dead anyway.

5
Resources – II

Feet Exercises

For the feet, I am going to refer you to *Steps of Faith* again. In the 'Make It Work' section in the centre of the book, Exercises 8 – 14 inclusive will provide a good combination of loosening and strengthening. To remind you:

Exercise eight: Brushes

Brush one foot along the floor, in front and behind, sixteen times. Swing it a little higher, so it just leaves the floor, sixteen times. Kick forward and back quite high, sixteen times.

Exercise nine: Pliés

These are knee bends, feet together and turned out, pushing the knees out over the toes as you go down. Do them with feet apart as well.

Exercise ten: Circling the leg

With one thigh lifted parallel to the ground, toes pointed, circle the lower leg four times in each direction. Both legs.

Exercise eleven: The ankle

Point and flex the foot, eight times, then circle it round keeping the leg straight. Both legs.

Exercise twelve: The instep

Flex the instep by pressing the toes of one foot into the ground and lifting the heel as high as it will go – eight times, both feet.

Exercise thirteen: The calf muscles

Slowly raise and slowly lower yourself by lifting both heels off the ground. Do it with feet together (turned out), and then with feet apart.

Face Exercises

The best way to do the face exercises is standing in the middle of the room in a circle facing each other. It's also more entertaining that way.

Stretch the features of the face as high and as wide as you can: raise the eyebrows, open the eyes wide, flare the nostrils, open the mouth, drop the jaw.

Then pull everything together – 'scrinch' your face as tightly as possible as if you are trying to make your eyebrows and your chin meet at your nose.

Stretch wide again;

'Scrinch' together;

Wide;

Together.

Alternate these another four times.

Make a chewing motion with your jaws, but keep your lips closed tight (don't bite your tongue).

Yawn – a big yawn – but keep your lips together from start to finish.

Take a breath and say 'oooooooooh', pushing your face and lips towards the centre of the circle.

Pull your head back and open your mouth wide and say 'aaaaaaaaaah'.

Lips forward, 'oooooooooh';

Head back, 'aaaaaaaaaaah';
Forward, 'oooooooh',
Back, 'aaaaaaaaah'.
Alternate: 'ooooooh' – 'aaaaaaaah' – 'ooooooooh' – 'aaaaaaaah'.
(Now work on your West Country accent!)

Raise and lower the eyebrows eight times.

Open the mouth wide (sideways, don't move the jaw), eight times.
Eyebrows up / down four times.
Mouth wide, four times.
Eyebrows twice, mouth twice, eyebrows twice, mouth twice.
Alternate eyebrows and mouth four times each.

Voice Exercises

Relaxation

Stand up straight.

Relax and ease the shoulders by lifting and dropping them alternately.

Then roll them around: pull them forward, lift them up to your ears, pull them back and lower them. Then reverse it: lower, pull back, lift up, pull forward. Repeat twice more each way.

Gently drop the head forward, then (gently) roll it round to the side, then back to the other side, then forward. Then reverse it, and roll it round the other way.

(Relaxed shoulder and neck muscles are essential for good voice production; this also holds true for sound-effects production.)

Breath control

Breathe in through the nose and out through the mouth. Push all of the air out of your lungs. Breathe in to a silent count of four, and out to a count of four. In for four, out for four. Then in for four, and out for six. In for four, out for six. Do the same thing in eights, then in twelves. Always take a rapid and full breath in, as silently as possible, but as freely in your head and chest as possible.

Then, with the lips lightly (not tightly) together, make a humming noise. Take a breath in through the nose, then breathe out through the nose as you hum. Try to hum strongly enough so that you feel a resonance in the sinus and nasal cavities, as well as making the lips tingle.

Articulation

Then work on the lips.

Take a big breath, and as long as you can while breathing out intone:

Ma-ma-ma-ma-ma, etc. Try to achieve the same resonance in the head as when humming.

Then:

Na-na-na-na-na-na-na etc.

Now, just the consonant sounds:
p p p p p p p p p p p p,

t t t t t t t t t t t.

suh suh suh suh suh suh suh suh suh suh suh suh

k k k k k k k k k k k k.

Then the same consonants, with vocalising, that is:

b b b b b b b b b b b b

d d d d d d d d d d d d

zuh zuh zuh zuh zuh zuh zuh

g g g g g g g g g g g g.

Then alternate:

p b p b p b p b p b p b ('puh-buh')

t k t k t k t k t k.

Finally, make the 'l' sound by dropping the tongue all the way from the roof of the mouth down to the floor of the mouth:

la la la la la la la.

Do it very slowly at first, then gradually speed it up.

Make the tongue travel all the way from the roof of the mouth to the floor, even when doing it very fast.

Cicely Berry's *Voice and the Actor* (Harrap: London, 1973) gives a professional introduction to the subject of voice and speech production. I also recommended *Anthology of British Tongue-Twisters* by Ken Parkin, (Samuel French: London, 1969).

PART 2

The Workshops

6

Workshop Summaries

1. Games: 'My Bonnie', 'Snoball-Noball'
   Basic Hand Exercises
   Manipulation – First principles
   Improvisation: Show an object
   Face Exercises, Snap Expressions
   Game: 'Pass the Face'.
2. Games: 'Knee-capping', 'The Different seat'
   Basic Hand Exercises
   Manipulation: Flat-Take, the *toc*
   Homework
   Feet Exercises
   Side-slip Step
   Slow-motion Cherry.
3. Basic Hand Exercises
   Manipulation: recap
   The Cube, Coat and Hat
   Homework
   Feet Exercises
   Profile Walk (I)
   Face Exercises; Snap Expressions
   Improvisation: Bus-stop.
4. Game: 'Red, Blue, Yellow'
   Basic Hand Exercises

Manipulation: +
Fixed Point
Floor pole, shelf, cane
Homework
Feet Exercises; Profile Walk (II)
Improvisation: Fixed Point in pairs.

5. Game: 'Buzz-Buzz'
   Hand Exercises
   Manipulation – two objects
   The Sphere
   Game: 'Snoball-Noball'
   Cane toss
   Homework
   Feet Exercises; Profile Walk (III)
   Improvisation: Occupations (I)
   Game: 'Chain Mime'.
6. Game: 'Knee-capping'
   Hand Exercises
   Manipulation: *Clic*, suitcase
   Improvisation: Heavy Item, in pairs.
   Feet Exercises; Pressure Walk.
   Face and Eye Exercises
   Eye Improvisation
   Occupations (II).
7. Game: 'Like *this*'
   Hand Exercises
   Manipulation: Rope and String Pull
   Homework
   Face Exercises
   Vocal Exercises
   Game: 'Pandora's Box'
   Improvisation: Modern Life.
8. Basic Hand Exercises
   Advanced Hand Exercises
   Face and Vocal Exercises

Game: 'Pandora's Box'
Homework
Game: Eye Contact
The Gaze
Improvisation: Gazes
Feet Exercises: Walks.

9. Game:'Hey Everybody.'
Hand Exercises, Basic and Advanced
Undulations
Homework
Improvisation: 'Comic Strip'
Feet Exercises; Practise Walks
Climbing Stairs
Mime Pictures.
10. Hand Exercises
Manipulation: A Brick
Face Exercises; Snap Expressions
Voice Exercises
Homework
Feet Exercises
Descending Stairs
Improvised rehearsal.

7
Workshop 1

After arrival, introductions, warming up by radiators, etc. and a word of prayer together, it will help everyone to relax if you begin with a game.

Game: 'My Bonnie'

Everybody stands in a circle and sings the song through once together.

My bonnie lies over the ocean
My bonnie lies over the sea
My bonnie lies over the ocean
Oh bring back my bonnie to me.
Bring back
Bring back
Oh bring back my bonnie to me, to me.
Bring back
Bring back
Oh bring back my bonnie to me.

Then introduce two quite different postures, of your own choosing. One could be standing with arms outstretched, leaning back on one leg, with the other heel forward, head back, as if singing a romantic aria. The other should be as different as possible, eg, in a crouch, knees bent, elbows tucked into sides, hands under chin.

The game is very simple. Start singing the song in the first position, change to the second when the '*b*' of bonnie is sung, and alternate very rapidly between the two positions, changing whenever a '*b*' is pronounced. The last line, for instance, involves three changes.

It gets quite fast and furious, demands concentration, and should be fun. Speed it up to sing it a second or third time.

Explanation

Explain the pattern of workshops to come, the kinds of work that will be covered, and what will be expected of the group.

Limber-up and Work-out

See pages 32–38. Limber up and do the work-out you have planned.

Finish with running in place very fast, then very slowly, then fast again, then with knees raised, then with heels raised behind – for a couple of minutes.

Or play a game of 'tag'.

Game: 'Snoball–Noball'

This is an introduction to handling imaginary objects.

Sitting in circles in groups of three to six, pass round from one to the next an imaginary ball the size of a soccer ball. As each person takes it and passes it on, he or she must pay close attention to exactly how it would feel, how heavy it is, its texture, etc. as well as being faithful to its size and shape in his or her hands. When the 'ball' has gone round once, the leader announces that it is made of something different, and the circle handles it accordingly. It could be:

a balloon
a glass globe
fluffy cotton wool
wet cotton wool
a shiny, hollow, stainless-steel ball
the same, but too hot to handle
a perfect sphere of ice
made of mud
an extremely sensitive explosive device
a melon covered in toffee.

Encourage everyone to 'feel' the ball in their hands. They should be concentrating as strongly as they can, so the game should be played without a lot of talking.

This should be fun. It also makes the point that, for all the technical skill required, mime starts with two things: imitation and imagination. Try to curb a little the natural tendency to fool around, so that each person has a chance to be aware of their own mental processes as they pass round the ball.

Technique

Do the Basic Hand Exercises (pp 38–40).

Introduce some of the principles of *Manipulation*, or handling imaginary objects, and talk about the mime techniques we are going to cover, especially:

Separation (or isolation) of Movements
Economy of Gesture
Fidelity to the shape of an object.

Separation of Movement

This means completing one action before beginning another, and dividing up an activity into small segments, each separated from the last by a very short pause. Obviously movement is infinitely divisible, but major limb movements and changes of direction are basically the points at which to pause. Take this to an extreme when practising. (For an example, see *Steps of Faith*, pp 42–43).

Economy of Gesture

This is related to the above, and sometimes comes as a by-product: only move those parts of the body that are strictly necessary to the action. For example, don't shuffle the whole body around to look at something, readjusting the position of arms, chest, head and neck, when a simple, clean turn of the head will do. Unless the characterisation calls for it, always cut out extraneous movement – and simplify, simplify, simplify.

Fidelity to the Shape of an object

This means more than just holding your hands in exactly the shape as they would be in for a real object. Their position must *define* the shape of the imaginary object for the audience. Secondly, the fingers must be *held strongly* in that position to help give the impression of the solidity of the object.

It also means paying attention to where other edges and surfaces would be, and keeping the object vividly in your mind for a good length of time after you have finished with it. It is a great shame to walk through something you've just been using when the audience is still 'seeing' it.

Everyone in the group does the following sequence together, with clear and precise separation of movement.

Take a glass from a shelf at eye level, as follows.
Arm up; arm out; hand open. Seize glass. Lift it.
Bring it towards you. Lower it down.
Put it down on a table at waist level. Release it.
Take a bottle (of whatever you want) from further away in front of you, and bring it closer.

Remove the top.
Pour out a drink into the glass. Replace the top.
Take a sip. Put it down again.

Try to think just what kind of glass you are handling, what shape it is and how heavy it is, and show that in your hand. Decide what is in the bottle, and how full it is – this will determine how you pour it out. Count the twists you give to the cap, and do the same number when you put it back on (don't forget where you put it down!). When you drink, tilt the glass only as much as you would when taking a sip of a real drink – it's not much – until the glass is quite empty. Give a real swallow . . . and enjoy the drink.

Improvisation

Everyone practises handling an imaginary object of their own for a few minutes, and then shows it to the rest of the class.

Face Work

Do the Face Exercises (p 47)

Introduce the following exaggerated expressions:

Raise the eyebrows, open the eyes wide, drop the jaw, and pull the lips forward into an 'o'. We'll call this 'surprise'. Make it as extreme as possible. Now relax the face. On a snap of the fingers, resume the expression, hold it for a few seconds, and on the next snap, relax.

Next raise the eyebrows, stretch the corners of the mouth as wide and pull them as high as possible, slightly squint the eyes, and call this one 'happy'. Relax, and then on the snap, put it on again.

On a snap of the fingers, resume 'happy', and on the next *snap*, relax. Then 'surprise', then relax. Alternate between these two states on cue, making each as extreme as you can, and freezing each one until the next signal.

Of course, these are nothing like expressions you would use on stage, they are merely for exercising the facial muscles.

Game

This is a facial version of Chinese whispers. Stand in a circle. The first person makes the most extraordinary expression he can think of, and holds it. He turns to the person on his left, who faces him and attempts to mirror not only the expression but also the whole posture resulting from this expression. When that person has succeeded (to the satisfaction of the other), he turns and 'gives' the face to the next one, who passes on what he sees, and so on.

Compare the first person's expression with the last, and see the variations that have crept in. Do this four or five times, giving different people the chance to start off, and changing the order of the circle occasionally.

If there is any time left, finish with a group activity such as Machines (see *Steps of Faith*, p 36).

Homework

Choose an imaginary object and use it naturally in two or three ways that will show what it is. Choose ways of using it that the audience are going to identify with as quickly as possible. Be economical with ideas, as well as with actions. Be ready to perform this at the next workshop.

8

Workshop 2

Stretch and limber-up
Run in place, or play a game of 'Knee-capping'.

Everyone runs around the room with a hand on each knee, 'protecting' their knee-cap. (It's more of a waddle, really.) The aim is to strike as many other knees as possible while guarding your own. If your knee is fairly struck, you must drop onto it (you may still reach for passing knees with the other hand). When both knees are struck, you are out and must remain kneeling where you are.

Obviously, too much caution inhibits the game. Stop when half the group are down and out, or everyone is gasping for breath, whichever comes first.

Game: 'The Different Seat'

Introduce the principle of *imagination*, and the motivation this supplies to movements, with the following game (adapted from Anna Scher's and Charles Verrall's *100+ Ideas for Drama* (Heinemann: London 1975).

Place an ordinary, strong chair, of the stackable plastic type, in the middle of one end of the room, facing everyone at the other end. One by one, they are to go up to the chair and sit down. As they sit down, or while they are sitting, they are to react with their body to some imaginary feature of the chair that you have told them about as they walked up to it. This should be done in silence. They then get up and exit in the opposite direction.

The reaction may be immediate and swift (such as to a drawing pin), or delayed and gradual. Either way it should not be forced and as far as possible not acted. Rather it should be a *re*action by the body, propelled by the imagination, to what is found. Nor should it be a complete mini-drama, telling a story – it is just a physical response, quite short in length.

Here are some possibilities:

a drawing pin
a pool of cold water
freshly painted (ask afterwards whether in the person's mind it was fresh, slippery, gloss paint, or was it drying out and a little tacky?)
covered in glue
grows mysteriously hot, becoming eventually too hot to touch
grows mysteriously cold, becoming absolutely icy
it is a throne
it is already occupied
it is the hardest seat in the world
it is the most comfortable
it is next to someone you dislike
it has a very strong smell
it has itching powder on it.

Everyone does this two or three times with a different title each time.

The leader should encourage subtle and truthful responses by repeating the requirements that people must not play-act for everyone else, nor should they get involved in a story. They must concentrate very hard on the imagined situation, not on their own reactions, and certainly not on the audience. Some reactions will take longer than others, but none should last longer than thirty seconds. Ask people to look, while they are watching, for truthful responses, and to notice what the whole body is 'saying', not just the face.

Manipulation

Do the Basic Hand Exercises (pp 38–40).

Introduce the concept of the Flat-Take (see *Steps of Faith*, p 43). This is a development of the separation of movement looked at last week. It is a technique to ensure that there is never any doubt in the mind of an audience about whether or not an imaginary object has been taken hold of or released. For absolute clarity, each part of the process is distinct and separated by a tiny pause. The hand is either very clearly empty or definitely forming the shape of the object it is supposed to be holding. (The lack of this technique is the cause of so many door handles appearing to be carried away and dropped somewhere in the room.)

The Flat-Take means that you always approach an object with the hand flat or wide open. Stop when you come into contact with the object, and after a tiny pause, take hold of it. After another tiny pause, lift it or turn it or whatever you are going to do with it.

The same principle applies when letting go. Stop for a moment before letting go, release the hand to wide open, stop again, them move the hand away.

Practise with a cupboard door. Remembering both separation and economy of movement, approach it, close fingers around the knob or handle, open it (move the hand in a smooth arc parallel to the floor), close it and let go. Then try opening and closing the doors at different heights.

The toc

The *toc* is the quality of movement that is used to show that your previously mobile, fluidly animate hand has come into contact with something concrete and solid. With the *toc* there is a small but definite explosion of energy at the end of a movement in the hand as it makes contact with an object. It is a kind of snap-stop, *after* which the hand conforms to the shape of the object.

Be sure to suit the scale of the *toc* to the size or mass of the object. If it is a wall your hands come up against, make the *toc* very strong and pronounced, with the fore-arms and even the shoulders coming into it. If it is, say, a thimble, the *toc* is still there, but it only involves your fingers. In fact, the *toc* should be present when any part of the body comes to rest against an imaginary object.

The *toc* is one of the fundamental elements of the mime of handling imaginary objects. It is vital to the magic of creating a solid reality out of thin air for the audience, and when mastered accounts for a lot of the pleasure that mime gives to watch. It must be a part of your movement whenever handling imaginary objects.

Practise this quality of movement first of all in the abstract. Make a series of flowing easy movements with the hands and arms, and then suddenly freeze all movements, with a marked tension and energy in the hands as they stop. After a couple of seconds, release the pose and flow again. Alternate these for several minutes, noting the contrast in the dynamic quality of what you are doing.

Then: handle a pole about three feet long suspended vertically in mid-air in front of you, as described in '*Steps of Faith*', pp 44. Separate all movements with tiny pauses as you open hand flat, approach it, flat – stop (*toc*) – take hold of it, first with one hand, then the other. Then turn it through 90° so that it is horizontal in front of you. Change the grip with each hand, one after the other, and continue turning it around another 90°. When it is vertical, stop. Release and bring one hand down, take hold and then bring the other hand up, and begin again.

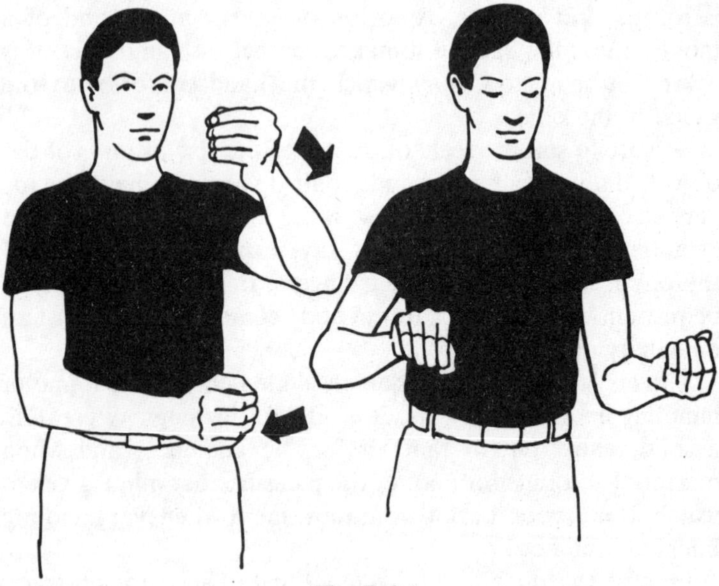

'The Pole'

The primary importance is not the sequence, but practising it with a simple object of regular dimensions. Make sure that

1. all movements are economical
2. all movements are separate
3. there is a *toc* when coming into contact with the pole
4. hands are faithful to the shape of it (look out for the little finger, which can turn it into a cone, and for the lack of alignment and rigidity in both hands, which leaves the

audience with the impression that what you have is a very large cooked spaghetti noodle)

5. movements are enlarged sufficiently to make it very clear that hands are moving around, and not through, the pole.

Practise this for five minutes more. Suggest that people split into pairs to help one another with accurate positioning of the hands around this imaginary pole.

Look at the Homework.

Do the Feet and Leg Exercises.

Practise the Sideways Slip-step (heel-toe-heel) walk in *Steps of Faith*, pp 61–2.

Finish with this slow motion exercise from Richmond Shepard's *Mime: The Technique of Silence* (Drama Book Publishers: New York, 1971).

Talk the group through the following sequence.

There is a bowl of cherries on a table in front of you. Bring your hands up one after the other, and down onto the table top, with a good *toc* and flat hand as you do so (are the hands level?). Each should use a point on their own anatomy, such as the hip bone, as a reference point.

Then flat – *toc* – take the side of the bowl. Each hand makes a 'shell' shape – *La Coquille*, remember?

One hand comes up and reaches down into the bowl. Stop.

Take the joined together stems of two cherries between thumb and forefinger, and lift them up to eye level. Bring up other hand, take one stem, and pull the cherries apart.

Lower one back into the bowl.

Bring the other to the mouth.

Take it on the tongue, draw it into the mouth. Close teeth.

Pull the stem away.

Release it, follow with the eyes as it falls to the floor.

Lift head up and front, then lower hand down.

Four or five chews. Stop.

Push stone to front of mouth. Remove with one hand.

Finish chewing. Swallow. (A look of ... delight, satisfaction, disgust, nausea or whatever comes/passes across the face.)
Stop, leaving hand with stone still in air.
Look to partner. Throw stone at them.
React to *their* stone speeding towards your forehead.
Freeze.

Everyone performs this, in pairs, for everyone else. Tell them to do it in strict slow motion and to remember all the principles covered. Be aware of your partner in case he or she finishes first and is winging a stone at your ear as you, quite oblivious, are still chewing your cherry. If the group is large, do it in fours. Afterwards point out major areas for individuals to concentrate on, if you wish, but by and large do not subject this work to criticism.

Homework

Bring in an imaginary object sequence as last week. Choose a new object, and practise performing it in three different ways: normal speed, twice the speed and with sharp angles and little stops, like a robot.

9
Workshop 3

Stretch and Limber-up.
End with running-in-place, or a game of 'tag'.

Manipulation

Do the Basic Hand Exercises (pp 38–40).

Recap the principles of manipulation that have been covered so far: Separation of Movement, Economy of Gesture, Fidelity, The Flat-Take and the *toc*.

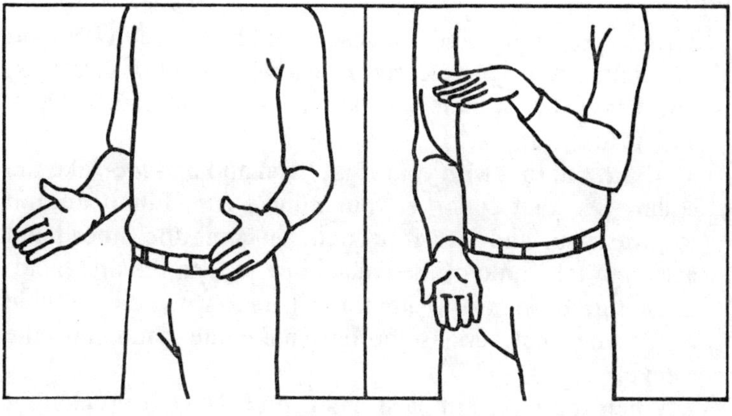

'The Cube'

Remember all these things as you practise the pole-handling sequence from the last workshop. Then practise with a large cube suspended in mid-air just in front of you (see *Steps of Faith*, p 45). Take hold of it by each of its faces. Then try twisting and turning it.

Try to take each face of the cube with a distinct movement that throws the hand flat and absolutely rigid as it hits the cube. Only move one hand at a time. This enables greater precision to be given to the movement; it also gives continuity to the object for the onlooker. Be strict with yourself – and with one another – pointing out where the hands are destroying the illusion of a perfect cube. Practise this for several minutes.

Along with technical proficiency, mime demands the development of an imaginative ability. The purpose of the 'Snoball' exercise in the first workshop, and of the 'Different Seat' game in the second, was to stimulate the imagination and stir the memory of how things actually feel to touch, hold, lift and handle.

Talk the class through the following sequence, emphasising the sense memory that is needed to mime truthfully.

> Turn to your right, and visualise a coat hung over a hook on the wall. See it very clearly. Know what kind of coat it is, how heavy it is, what it is made of, what colour it is and how well it fits you.
>
> Reach out to it with your right hand and flat- *toc*- take the collar. See that collar in your mind's eye. Lift it up and towards you, and turn it around, reaching the other hand across to take hold of the collar. Let go with the first hand, draw it in towards you, aim the fingers towards the armhole inside the coat, and smoothly snake the hand into the sleeve.
>
> When the right arm is straight, pull the coat up along it and over the shoulder to the neck. Release the collar.

Reach behind with the left hand and, after a couple of tries, find the other sleeve. Slide the arm in until it is straight, bring it around in front. Finally, throw the coat onto the shoulder with a quick lift if it is quite a heavy coat. Pull it up with the hands on either side of the collar if it is not.

If you leave out this last tiny movement you have left out a movement that is virtually universal – in cold northern countries anyway – and the audience will never feel comfortable until you do it properly. By this I mean that they are not going to be physically at ease. Try it for yourself. Put on the coat, as before, but after you slide your arms into the sleeves, simply lower your shoulders and drop your arms to your side. Feel something missing? Anyone watching would. This is just a tiny illustration of the kind of physical identification that happens between a mime and an audience.

Then put on a hat, with the same imagination of all its details and attention to how it feels to put it on.

Now look at the homework.

Do the Feet and Leg Exercises.

Practise the Side Step walk (from last week) for a few minutes.

If people have mastered it, put them into pairs and practise doing it in perfect synchronisation, arm in arm. They should keep the upper halves of their bodies frozen, and glide along with the feet, heel-toeing along.

Then start work on the Profile walk-without-changing-place (see *Steps of Faith* pp 58–61).

Don't try to do it all at once. First work on smoothly stepping out with one leg while balancing on the other. The foot should come up and out in a small bicycling motion, but however large the step, the foot finishes up with the heel one inch from the ground.

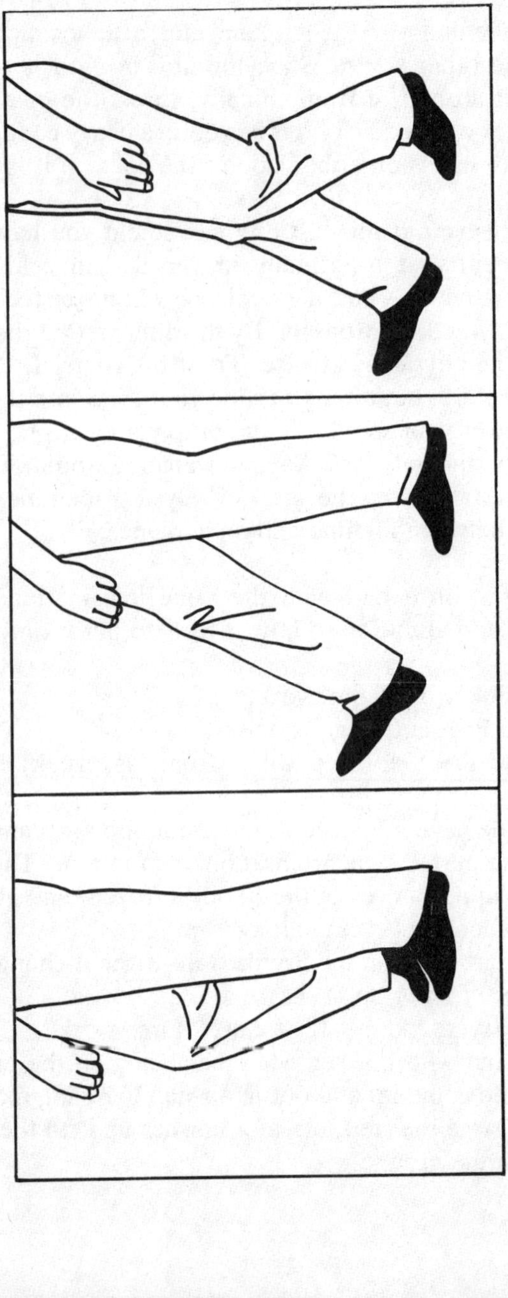

start step pull

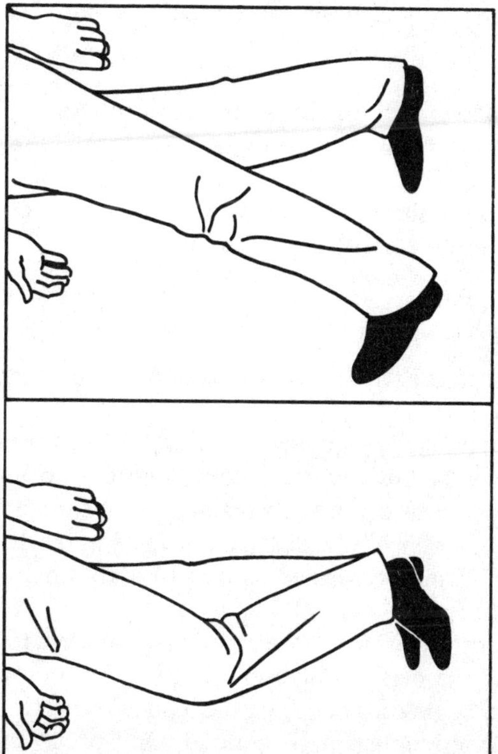

step

finish/start

Then practise the lifting-heel-while-drawing-knee-forward of the supporting leg. Eventually, combine that with pulling the straight leg back into place, and you are in position for another step of the walk.

Leave the hands and arms until another time.

Do the Face Exercises and practise Snap Expressions, adding:

> Angry: lower jaw forward, corners of mouth pulled down, eyebrows down in a frown.
>
> Proud/snobbish: eyebrows raised, eyes half closed, jaw down, mouth closed, upper lip long.

Improvisation

Finish with the Bus-stop demonstrations (see *Steps of Faith*, p 37).

Let each person's sequence of actions at a bus stop be about twenty seconds. Give everyone four minutes to work out what they are going to do, and to practise it. It should be simple enough to be repeated exactly the same way each time, and capable of being performed as part of a continuous cycle of movement.

Ask four to six of the more confident members to stand in a line across the performing area. Starting from perfectly still, they are to begin on a cue from the leader and go through that sequence continuously until stopped. On a prearranged signal from the leader, they all stop and freeze in whatever position they have reached. After a pause of a couple of beats, one of them, chosen beforehand, starts moving again and carries on doing their sequence a few times more until stopped by the leader.

Ask them all to stay up in front of the others while the exercise is discussed. The following questions may be asked:

1. Which was the most interesting sequence to watch?
2. To whom was your eye drawn. Why?
3. Did the position in the line matter? What kinds of things drew the eye? Clothing or colours being worn? Size? One man among a line of women, or vice versa?
4. Did certain movements catch the eye?
5. Did anyone manage to watch any sequence all the way through?
6. Why not? (If anyone did, how did they do it?)
7. Where was the focus of attention when all but one were stopped?

It may seem obvious, but drive home the point that if an action is important, no other movement must distract from it, and in mime, action is important.

For every moment in a piece of mime, there must be one, and only one, focus of attention. This is where you intend the audience to pay attention, and where they have to pay attention if they are going to follow what is happening. Just as in a play when only one person can speak at a time if the dialogue is going to be understood, so the focus of attention must be transferred smoothly from one mime on stage to another, or if solo, from one part of the body to another.

Homework

Bring in a pair of imaginary objects of very different sizes, such as a large box with a needle and cotton inside, and handle them clearly and with *toc*s, etc.

10

Workshop 4

Game: 'Red, Blue, Yellow' (from *Acting: A Drama Studio Source Book*)

Each member of the group gets a chair swiftly, and sits in a circle with a space between each chair. The tutor quickly gives each person in the circle a colour, alternating between red and blue. The tutor explains that the purpose of the exercise is precise movement, with no fuss, and in complete silence. On the order 'Red'!', all the Reds must rise and find another chair. On the order 'Blue!', all the blues have to find another chair. On the order 'Yellow!', everyone finds another chair. Vary the manner in which the movement is to be carried out, from lightning reaction to slow motion. No contact may be made, and the transfer from one chair to another must be made with a minimum of movement. Start giving the orders slowly and then speed up to get very quick reactions.

Stretch and Limber-up

Finish with a game of 'Tag', 'Dog and bone', or 'Red Rover'.

Do the Basic Hand Exercises.

Practise Manipulation, remembering all the things covered

so far, with an imaginary object in the shape of a 'plus' sign (+), and having the same thickness and length as the pole used in the second week. Turn it and twist it, always aiming for *precision* and *fidelity* in the minutest detail. Explore the possibilities of manipulating this object.

The Fixed Point

While the solidity of objects is conveyed very pleasingly by the *toc*, their immobility is conveyed by a technique known as the Fixed Point. Like the *toc*, this is one of the most important concepts to master in manipulation technique. The Fixed Point is the ability to leave one part of the body, typically the hand, at a point in space while moving the rest of the body relative to it. From the view of the audience, the hand does not move in the slightest.

To practise the Fixed Point, take hold of an imaginary pole that stands vertically, running from floor to ceiling. Walk towards it. Walk away from it. The hand must not move relative to the floor, and the wrist must bend so that the hand does not rotate around the pole either. This may prove more difficult than it sounds. If so, work in pairs to practise.

Your partner holds a forearm up vertically, while you use this as your 'pole'. Grasp it tightly at first, and practise moving around it; then more loosely; then grasp a pole which is a quarter of an inch bigger all around than the arm, so that you do not touch your partner. Finally use just your partner's index finger as a reference point in space for your pole.

The Fixed Point should also be practised with hands placed flat on an imaginary shelf or table top. After the *toc* of making contact, move forward and back and from side to side. Then try keeping the hands on the same level while the rest of the body makes a smooth descent, bending the knees as you sink to the floor. Your hands will be up around the chin somewhere. Come back up, just as smoothly, with the hands just as fixed.

The Fixed Point

'. . . keeping the hands on the same level, while the rest of the body makes a smooth descent.'

Finish the manipulation work by handling a cane. Use your imagination to see it very clearly in all its detail: its material, weight, texture and finish. As you lower it, remember the *toc*, which must be seen in the hand as the tip hits the floor. Try leaning on it. Make sure that the line of the cane is continuous with the line of the arm. The arm must be very straight, and if the cane is vertical, the arm should be as well. In that case, you will need to lift your shoulder as you lean, so that the cane doesn't appear to compress.

Now look at the homework.

Do the Feet Exercises.

Practise the walks we have looked at so far. When you come to the Profile Walk, stress the importance of bending the knee *and* lifting the heel of the supporting leg at the same time, not one after the other (all the weight is being lifted by the calf muscles – not easy!). That happens while the leg extended straight in front is being drawn stiffly back.

Practise moving the arms. They are not rigid and mechanical but there is a regularity to their movement, as well as a pause between each swing. This pause coincides with the stepping-out of the leg that is opposite the arm that is forward. Remember that the hands always move *in opposition* to the legs, as they do in normal walking.

Improvisation – Fixed Point

In pairs, create a one-and-a-half minute piece in which you establish an object together, and return to it individually, each making sure it is in the same place for the audience as the other character left it. It could be a stove two cooks are using, or a ship's handrail two passengers are leaning on. Spend ten minutes working it out. Each pair shows the rest of the class what they have done.

Homework

Create a sequence that involves handling an imaginary object during which it stops working properly. Try to show exactly what has gone wrong and when.

11
Workshop 5

Stretch and Limber-up.

Game: 'Buzz-Buzz' (from *Acting: A Drama Studio Source Book*)

This warming-up exercise encourages observation, inventiveness, freedom of physical expression and the feeling of ensemble.

> In this exercise, the whole group are jogging about in the studio space. The tutor has a buzzer or something that makes a strident noise. When the buzzer sounds, everyone freezes and looks at a 'victim' at whom the tutor points. The tutor buzzes again and the 'victim' instantly acquires his own extraordinary movement routine and leaps into action. Immediately all the group are affected in the same way. The action continues for, say, ten seconds, then the tutor buzzes again, everyone freezes and the tutor points to another 'victim'.
>
> Stop the exercise before people start to flag.

Manipulation

Do the Basic Hand Exercises (p 38).

Practise two of the previous manipulation exercise objects: choose between a pole, a 'plus' sign, a cube, a glass or a cherry. Recap the principles covered so far: Separation of Movement, Economy of Gesture, Fidelity to Shape, the Flat-take, the *toc*, the Fixed Point.

Then work with a sphere. Imagine it is suspended in mid-air in front of you. Whereas you approached the cube with a slightly open hand, and snapped into a perfectly flat hand, be sure the hand approaching the sphere is quite wide open, nearly flat. After the *toc* that brings the whole arm to rest, the hand assumes, with a sharply defined movement, the shape of the shell – *La Coquille* – about half a beat later. The other hand does likewise. When comfortable with that process of taking it and letting it go, (one hand at a time), and retaking it at different positions on the 'ball', practise turning and rotating it.

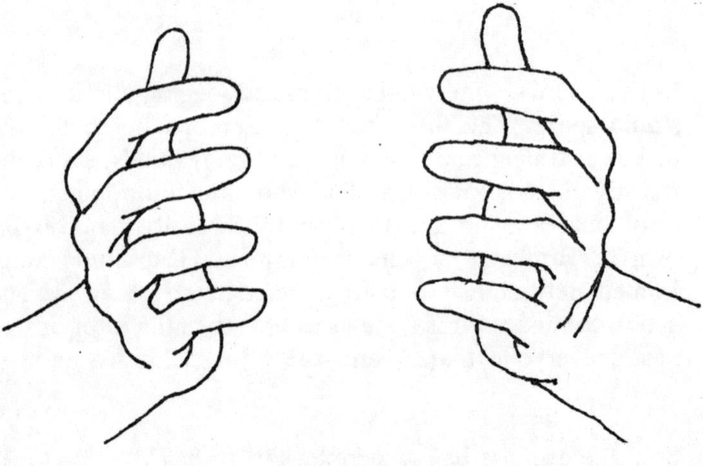

The Sphere

Split into groups of three, four or five and do the 'Snoball-Noball' exercise from the first Workshop, paying much more attention this time to the accuracy of manipulation without losing the inspiration provided by free imagination.

Come together again and practise manipulating a cane for a few moments. Then practise tossing it lightly from one hand to the other. In this action it is more important than ever that the Flat-*toc*-Take is executed very quickly as the cane is caught. Prepare to catch the cane with a completely flat hand, show the impact with a sharp move backwards (giving with it in the direction of travel), and close around it as the hand stops. When throwing, be sure the arm finishes its motion with the hand very obviously wide open. As you vary the 'force' used in throwing and catching, the speed of the toss varies, and so does the time interval between the two actions. Note the difference between tossing it high into the air, giving with the catch by moving the hand downwards and throwing it straight across from hand to hand: the give is almost completely in the horizontal.

Look at the homework.

Do the Face Exercises.

Do the Feet and Leg Exercises.

Practise the Profile Walk (see *Steps of Faith*, pp 58–61). If it is going well for people, ask them each to demonstrate their version in turn to the rest of the group. Try to make one or two helpful criticisms and suggestions to improve each walk.

Improvisation: Occupations

Devise a sequence to convey the essence of an occupation or profession, as explained in *Steps of Faith*, p 51. Let each one show their sequence to the rest of the group.

Game: 'Chain Mime'

A minimum of five people are required to play this game. Send out between three and five people from the room, and give one of the remaining people the subject of a short activity to be mimed, such as changing a baby's nappy, or writing and posting a letter. One peson is then called in to watch while this is mimed. As soon as this is finished, a second person is called in to watch the first person perform their version of what they thought the original mime was. They then perform *their* version to the third person, who performs it for the next, and so on. There should be no guessing or comments on the mimes until the last person has come in and performed. Starting with the last, ask each to say what activity they were miming. It's like a mime version of 'Chinese Whispers'. Try it two or three times.

Homework

Rework your occupation, if necessary, to take note of criticisms and advice. Make sure its length is down to 20–25 seconds.

12
Workshop 6

Stretch and Limber-up.

Game: 'Knee-capping' (see Workshop 2)

Manipulation

Do the Basic Hand Exercises (p 38).

The principle to look at today is the *clic*. This refers to a visible moment of preparation by the body for a strenuous action such as lifting or pushing. It is not a movement, but a kind of stiffening or tensioning that occurs in between placing the hands or arms, etc. in position and actually moving them. It lasts a split-second, but it signals to the audience that the effort involved in the following action is going to be considerable.

> Put the *clic* into the sequence of actions involved in: reaching down, picking up, walking two steps with and putting down a heavy suitcase. After putting it down, relax the *clic*, in a separate moment, before releasing your grip and pulling the hand away.

Another way of describing the *clic* is: the force necessary to overcome the inertia of a stationary object. The harder it is (in reality) to move, the more pronounced will be this movement of effort that occurs just before it does move. Of course, if the object is completely immovable, then the *clic* just grows until the strain shows in every sinew, or the mime gives up.

Improvisation

Work out a short (two minute) sketch in pairs, in which an extremely heavy or reluctant object or animal is handed over from one person to another. Don't neglect character, but don't make the plot too complicated either.

Exercises

Do the Feet Exercises.

Practise the Walks so far.

Begin work on the Pressure Walk – *Marche en face*, or facing an audience (see *Steps of Faith*, pp 62–4).

Do the Face Exercises.

Follow with these Eye Exercises.

Keeping the head and face immobile, look as far as possible to the left, then to the right, to the left and again to the right.

Do the same twice as fast.

Look up, then down, then up, then down.

And again, twice as fast.

Starting with the eyes fully swivelled to the left, roll them up and around to the right, then down and around to the left. Roll them around again, and repeat twice going the opposite direction.

Turn the eyes to the left, focusing on something in the room, then turn the head to face that object; bring the eyes centre, then face centre.

Same thing to the right, then up, then down. Repeat, in all directions.

Do the Eye Improvisation (telling a story using just the eyes) from Richard Shepard's *Mime: The Technique of Silence*, quoted in *Steps of Faith*, pp 34–5.

Occupations

Everyone recalls and rehearses their occupation from last week, incorporating any improvements they feel are necessary. Give out a new set of occupations, let everyone choose one and work on it by themselves for ten minutes. At the end of that time, ask them to choose between the two that they have done, for further work. It would help if the length of each person's sequence is roughly the same, about twenty-five to thirty seconds. Encourage drastic pruning if necessary.

Here is a list of occupations (feel free to add to it):

Hairdresser/barber	Concert pianist
Waiter/tress	Shoplifter
Telephonist	Inventory/stock taking
College lecturer	Painter – artist
Painter – decorator	Lifeguard
Tailor/dressmaker	Nightwatchman
Milkman	Traffic warden

Go through the sequence twice without stopping. Freeze.

Go through it once in slow motion.

Go through it with little tiny pauses between each action.

Go through it at double speed.

Go through it with enormous effort, as if submerged in treacle.

Go through it as if you are on the moon (one-sixth your normal weight).

Shrink all the movements down.

Expand them so that all objects, etc. are twice as large as normal.

Rest for a minute.

Now try it in different moods or states of mind.

dreamily or preoccupied
angrily
forgetfully (pausing as if trying to remember the job at hand)
as if bored
in love
in pain
anxiously
enthusiastically.

For each of these last eight, encourage everyone to find a thought, a situation or an idea that will motivate them, and tell them to fix their minds on that as strongly as possible. They should know their routine by now. It is an opportunity to leave the technique to look after itself and to work on the actor's belief.

Actually it is a kind of dual concentration, in which the mime is completely aware of what is happening physically with his body, but he is also involved emotionally – in a theatrical sense – in the scene that is being played.

Homework

Create a character who has the same occupation you have just been working with. Give him or her an age, a name, and a bit of background. Decide on marital status, religious belief and conduct, general state of mind and a character trait or tendency. Imagine that they are just getting ready to go out to a meeting that they expect will have a profound effect on their future. Bring in a mime (length: one to two minutes) on the way they do the last few things before leaving the house.

13
Workshop 7

Stretch and Limber-up.

Game: 'Like *this* . . .'

An adaptation of 'Buzz-Buzz' played in Workshop 5.

Everyone runs randomly around the room. At a given signal from the leader, all look at him and freeze. The leader chooses one person by pointing. All the others turn to look at the first person, who must invent an extraordinary way of running and begin charging around the room, adding an equally extraordinary sound to go with the action. Immediately, and with *maximum* energy and commitment, all the others imitate this. They carry on until the leader stops this with the signal, after ten seconds or so, and points to another, who invents a new way of running and a new sound to go with it. Everyone immediately joins in, and so on. Stop before the energy flags.

Do the Basic Hand Exercises.

Follow with the Wrist Exercises.

Manipulation: String and Rope Pulling

The wrist action in the Wrist Exercises is a vital key to the illusion of pulling string or rope. The wrists *lead* the action in order to show more clearly the forces that are working. As you pull on a string the wrists lead in order to show the resistance of the string against your pull. As the string pulls you, the wrists lead in that direction, away from you, to show where the force is coming from. If you didn't do this, there would be a lessening of the illusion of a taut line stretched between your hands and extending beyond you.

Practise with a kite string. Imagine the kite string is running across the front of you from your lower right to your upper left. Grasp it with two or three fingers and the thumb, reach up with your left hand to take hold of it. As you reach across and up with your right hand, do not twist the shoulders to face the kite – keep facing the audience. Just reach across you as far as you can and take hold of the 'string'. (See illustration.)

Kite Pulls

Keeping the hands the same distance apart (that's the tricky bit), pull them down along the diagonal. Let go of the right hand first, reach over (don't twist the torso) and take hold just above the left hand, then move that hand, reach up and out with it to carry on. Remember the *clic* (a small one) as you prepare to pull against a little wind resistance.

Try letting the kite pull the arms up. This time the wrists lead in the upward direction.

The same principles apply to pulling rope, and to an imaginary tug of war. The best effect is obtained by facing front with the rope imagined to be running across in front of you at hip level. Reach across you with your right hand as far as possible (do not twist the body), and take hold of the rope, next to your hip-bone (illustration 1). Then reach out as far as possible with the left arm without bending or leaning towards the left, and take hold. As you are reaching with the left hand, let the hips slide in the opposite direction (illustration 2). Your hands, hips and shoulders stay exactly where they are, relative to the floor; your hands, of course, must be in line with your rope.

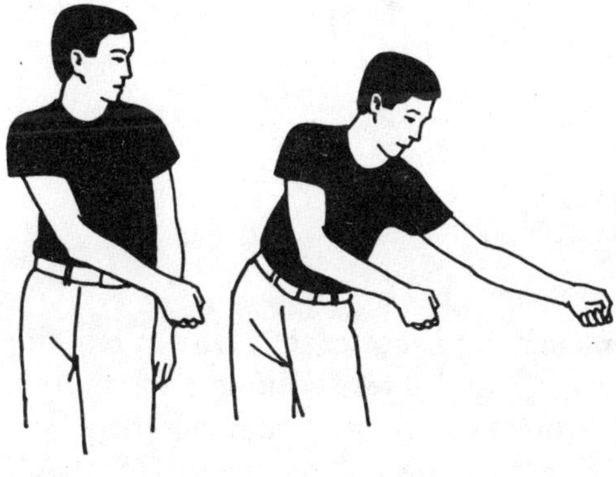

(1) (2)

Rope pulls

When you are fully extended, give a *clic* and pull on the rope, showing the resistance that you are encountering. As you pull the rope in, slide your hips across so that your left wrist comes to a stop against your hip-bone (illustration 3). Reach out and retake the rope, first with the right hand (illustration 4) then with the left (illustration 5). As you reach out with the left hand, slide the hips away back to the other side. (By all means look with your head in the direction of the rope, but remember to keep the chest facing front.)

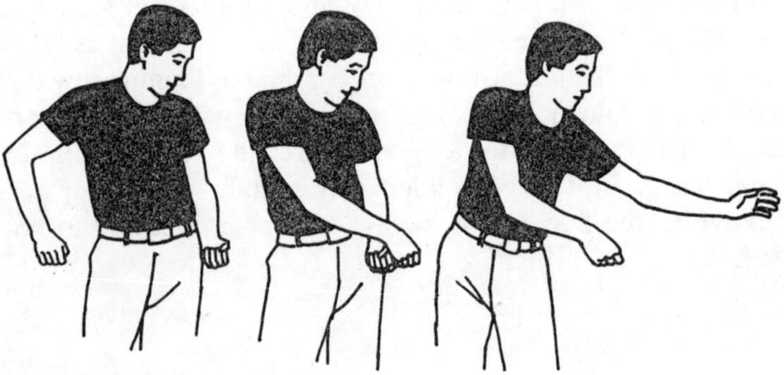

(3) (4) (5)

Rope pulls

The hip movement is not exactly true to real-life strenuous haulage of rope, but it does accentuate the movement of the hands and arms as they go past, and therefore helps the illusion of the rope going past the body. This is an example of 'body echo'. The dynamic of the hip movement must match the arms – very strongly, deliberate and against resistance when pulling, but more rapid and even surreptitious when reaching out with the hands and changing grip.

Look at the Homework.

For the remainder of the session, work on techniques of what is sometimes called 'mime theatre.' For an introduction to this, read the section on mime theatre in Appendix 1.

Start with Face Exercises.

Then move on to the Vocal Exercises.

Game

Play another round of 'Like *this* . . .', encouraging the group to let themselves go vocally as well as physically, and to aim at some really unusual sounds.

Game: 'Pandora's Box'

Imagine that you have in front of you a box, about a metre on each side, and in it is every animal in the world. As you open it, the noise of one particular animal is heard – it continues for four or five seconds until you slam the lid down, cutting off the sound abruptly. Try to *project* the sound with all the confidence you can muster, and try to *synchronise* the sound with the action of the lid. Remember to be precise in handling the box, being very clear with the movements.

Every member of the group should open the box in turn, and go round two or three times, trying not to repeat any animals. It will be difficult for some to do this exercise without feeling very silly, but encourage everyone to have a go, if at all possible.

Improvisation

Everyone chooses a couple of ordinary objects or activities from the list below – or others they might think of – and works on very short sequences in which they use these objects while making appropriate sounds. Each need last only ten to fifteen seconds.

Automatic washing-machine	Arcade machine video
Coffee-maker	Typewriter
Hoover	Paddling noise of a word-processor keyboard
Electric kettle	Computer printer
Tumble-drier	Telephone ringing
Car starting	Frying bacon and eggs
Bath running	Fish and chip shop
Thunderstorm	Train passing
Electronic till (reading bar codes on groceries with an electric eye)	Sawing a plank of wood
Wimbledon on TV	Bus or council refuse lorry as it reverses into your car

These sequences should be presented very quickly one after another, without comment or criticism. Each person announces their object or activity and then performs it. Keeping it moving, and give people a safe situation to fail if they need it.

If there is time left, allow people to start on the homework before going home.

Homework: 'A little louder, please'

The aim of this exercise is to develop freedom and imagination in vocal effects.

Each person must devise a thirty-second sequence of mimed actions, such as brushing teeth, or making a cup of coffee. When the movements are fixed, the sequence is performed with as many sounds added as possible – almost a continual stream of noises, based on the idea of an amplification of normally inaudible sounds (normal audible sounds should be very loud). For example hand moves towards toothpaste tube (whoosh), closes around it (soft thump), other hand approaches cap (whoosh), takes it between thumb and forefinger (click), unscrews it (creak, cree-eak) puts it down (whoosh, craack), etc.

Don't get hung up on particular sounds – keep making noises in order to maintain the energy level, even at the risk of repeating yourself. Keep the mime precise.

There are the following variations:

1. Work in slow motion.
2. Accentuate cinematic effect as if sound track is far too loud.
3. Repeat normal sequence at double speed.

14
Workshop 8

Stretch and Limber-up

End with Tag, Knee-capping, Buzz-Buzz.
Do the Basic Hand Exercises.
Introduce the Advanced Hand Exercises (p 41).
Do the Face and Vocal Exercises as last week.

Game: Pandora's Box

Play a variation on the game from last week.

1. Add the noise of a key turning in the lock before opening the box. Add a creaking hinge to the opening of the lid.

Or,

2. Open a door instead of a box, behind it is every form of transport known to man. Find a characteristic sound for each e.g. an ambulance, a horse (walking, trotting, galloping), a Model-T Ford, a locomotive, etc.

Look at the Homework.

Game: Eye Contact (Desmond Jones)

Divide into groups of four–six. All kneel or sit on the floor. Each person takes it in turn to stand in front of the rest of group, about two metres away, and keep up a continuous monologue. It can be on any subject from 'The most boring thing I did today' to 'Why I have no confidence in the present government'. As they are talking, each member of their group should slowly raise a hand from their lap to straight up, to a silent count of ten. Whenever the speaker looks one of them straight in the eye, they drop their hand and start again. The aim of the speaker is of course to prevent anyone from fully raising their hand.

Adjust the speed of the hand-raising so that it is neither too easy, not too difficult to achieve this. Instruct everyone to set high standards, so that the speaker feels they must maintain good eye contact with each and every person in their group. A quick glance will not do – the person must feel they have been genuinely addressed.

Let everyone in the group have a turn.

Improvisations

There is a mime convention called 'the gaze' in which the action is stopped momentarily and the expression of the actor(s) is deliberately and quite unmistakably delivered or presented to the audience. This is usually achieved by a quick, sharp head movement, a turn of the face to the audience, as all other action ceases. The look lasts one second – no less, and seldom more – before the head turns back and the action resumes. As a device it is like the Shakespearean 'aside', in which an actor breaks from the scene and comes downstage slightly in order to take the audience into his confidence or reveal his inner thoughts.

Enter and walk across the stage from stage left.

As you reach the centre, notice, stop, and look at something directly in front of you (between eye-level and the ground). Whatever it is causes your expression to change.

Freeze, then turn your head to the audience to show this expression (give them your eyes!) Don't rush it and do not alter your expression at all during this. The gaze should be directed above the head of the last row of the audience then everyone feels included.

Snap the head back and carry on. Deal with the object, preferably in some way that can show the audience what it is.

Each person should try this at least twice. Run them through quite quickly, especially the first time, without stopping to criticise, but encourage everyone to take time over it and not to be shy. The two most common mistakes are: (1) getting confused over the order of the movements, and (2) rushing it, or funking the look altogether out of shyness. Try to help everyone over these hurdles with gentle encouragement and by repeating the exercise as often as necessary.

Do the Feet Exercises and practise the walks.

If there is time, let people start on the homework for next week.

Homework

Devise a short sequence with as many sound effects as possible, in which something very small is seen to have enormous effects or consequences. You may wish to offer people the opportunity to work in pairs, if that is practicable for them during the week.

The group might like to bear in mind that this exercise describes the parable of the mustard seed (Matt 13) and that what they are looking for is a modern equivalent. Don't let them get bogged down in a discussion over the interpretation of Scripture. They should concentrate instead on telling a very simple story in mime, with a beginning, middle and end, and leave the interpretation to the audience. After all the pieces have been performed, you can then have a discussion about whether any could be seen as modern-day parables that carry a spiritual message in the right context.

15
Workshop 9

Stretch and Limber-up

Game: 'Hey, Everybody'

(Thanks to Pip and Rachel Hawthorn)
This game must be played with maximum energy and total, child-like commitment. It is great for an attack of the 'blah's' and, in an extremely silly way, draws a group together.

Form a circle on the floor, kneeling, crouched forward quite close together, and begin lightly but rapidly patting the floor with your hands, alternating to get a very fast rhythm. From this expectant and eager circle, one person shouts out, 'Hey, everybody!'

Immediately the patter ceases, and all answer as one, 'Yes?'

The initiator then makes a suggestion of any simple but bizarre or silly action he can think of. For example, 'Let's . . . all be chickens.'

The group replies, with undisguised joy in their voices at this absolutely wonderful idea: 'Yes! Let's!'

They then proceed to cluck and crow and flap their arms for all they're worth. After about 5 seconds, all quickly return to the circle and resume patting the floor, gleefully anticipating the next utterly thrilling suggestion. It always takes the same pattern:

'Hey everybody!' (Patting ceases.)
'Yes?'
'Let's . . . lie on our backs and kick our feet in the air!'
'Yes! Let's!'

Suggestions may come from anyone. Stop the game before the energy flags.

Do the Hand Exercises, Basic and Advanced.

Look at the homework.

Improvisation: 'Comic Strip'

(Thanks to Pip Hawthorn, and *The Gamester's Handbook*)
The aim of this game is to foster precise movement and economical story-telling in mime.

Divide into pairs or threes. Each group has four minutes to decide on an incident or a theme and to work out a series of four to six still pictures, each held for a few seconds to convey that. The convention they use with the audience, who close their eyes before the start of the 'strip', is to give them the title, and then to tell them when to open and when to close their eyes in order to view each scene.

The pieces should be performed in complete silence.

Sample titles could be:

An accident in the kitchen.
The examination.
The rich man and Lazarus.
Samson and Delilah.
Telling a joke.

A variation is to allow limited conversation, or sound effects, to be added, as long as there is no movement about the scene.

Do the Feet Exercises
Practise a walk briefly.

Technique: Climbing Stairs

The Feet.

Stand sideways on to an audience, feet together. Lift up the left foot, keeping it relaxed, then flex it as you step out and place it down a few inches in front of the right, toes on the ground, heel raised, knee bent. Lean forward slightly so that most of the weight is on that foot.

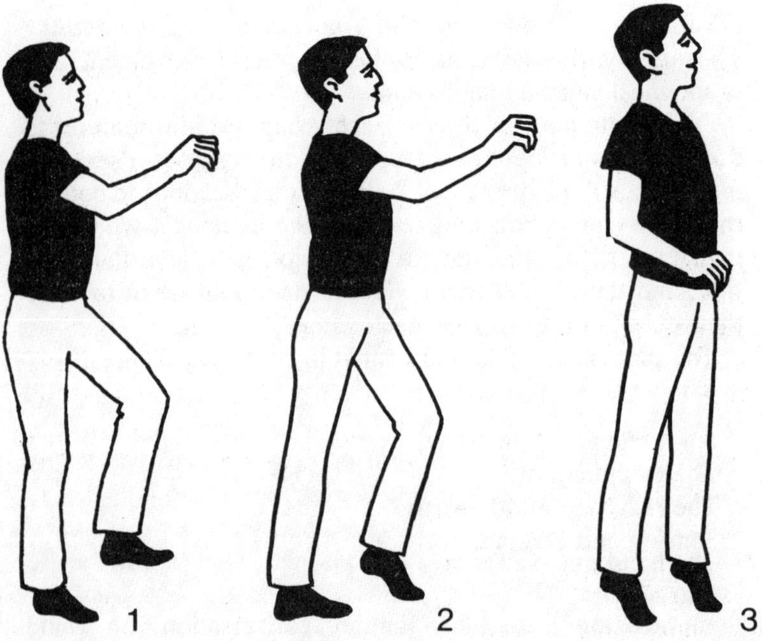

Climbing stairs

Now rise up sharply onto the balls of both feet, straightening the front leg. Stop.

Then gently and smoothly lower yourself down, bending the knee of the right leg. The right heel stays up, but the front leg is now straight, and all your weight is on it.

Even as you are lowering yourself down, prepare to take a step forward with the other leg, bringing it from behind and placing it down, heel raised, knee bent, as if you were stepping onto the next stair. Stop. Lean forward onto it, sharply raise yourself up, lower yourself down, switching the knee/heel that is bent/raised, etc.

These are the two halves of the climbing movement with the feet.

The Hands

The hand action is co-ordinated with the rise, but it is easier to practise it separately at first. Usually the hand furthest from the audience stays at your side. The other hand reaches up and takes a handrail. It moves down on the diagonal by the same amount with each rise, and it stays still as you take a step.

Imagine that the handrail runs from chest height (about an arm's length away) to hip height, in a straight line of course. Reach out and flat-*toc*-take it in front of you, at shoulder height. Pull it down a third of the way and stop. Pull it another third, and stop. Pull it the last third, so that the hand is level with your hip. Stop. Pull a bit further, release it with your hand, and reach up and begin the sequence again. With the three pulls and the pull–release–reach, you should be able to do it to a regular count of four.

The hand must describe a straight rail. Although the angle is exaggerated, the action of taking, pulling and releasing this rail must be exact and precise.

The feet and hands are combined by pulling down a segment of the rail each time you rise up on the balls of the feet, and staying still while you lower one heel and take the next step.

You travel forward, a step at a time, with this one.

Be sure that the upward movement is sharp and 'accented', because that is the part you want the audience to notice. The lowering down is meant to be subtle – it has a different dynamic quality altogether. When you rise up, your whole body must say, 'I am climbing up a step.' When you lower down, your chest and face are still climbing, and you are disguising the fact that your body is actually going down by simultaneously taking the next step, ie, bringing the back leg forward and putting it on the next stair. Remember above all that the illusion is only complete when you, the actor, are climbing stairs in your imagination. Look up to where you are going, and think about why you are going there – if you don't believe, the audience never will.

The rest of the session can explore the presentation of simple, immediate images or pictures that are capable of a symbolic interpretation. For an explanation read Appendix 2: Mime in public and private worship. Then give everyone the challenge of improvising a solo mime picture or image that they can then explain as symbolic of a spiritual or moral truth. They can try to interpret the pictures I've given as illustrations or make up their own. Note that it is not a sketch or a story, but a single, simple image that you want to give people.

Above all else, there is a need for simplicity. Remember – KISS (Keep It Short and Simple), both dramatically and theologically. Some of the parables Jesus told are very clear and straightforward, whereas others are immensely difficult to interpret and to understand fully. Do yourself a favour and go for the former type.

The presentation should be very short – ten to fifteen seconds, very rarely over a minute. Spoken introductions are allowed.

After people have had ten minutes to prepare, come together and share the ideas in a more informal way than usual, like a round-table discussion. Invite anyone to start the ball rolling, and don't insist that everyone must have a go. Discuss as a group what might work and what wouldn't. Try to keep the discussion from becoming too theological. You should know each other well enough by now.

If this looks like ending the evening in total confusion and uncertainty, fnish with a group activity such as Machine or Chain mime (see p 84).

Homework

Devise a brief mime sequence that creates an environment. Using a combination of manipulation, quick character and occupation mimes, and mimed sound effects, give the audience a sense of where you are.

The key is to move very quickly from one thing to the next, so that you build up an impression in people's minds by giving them as many clues in the quickest and most entertaining way possible. For example. In the home of a busy mother, with toddlers and babies all about, you would probably want to spend about five seconds on each of the following: cooking, washing up, hoovering, loading and putting on the washing machine (draw it and make its sounds), baby crying, or crawling and getting into things, telephone ringing.

16
Workshop 10

Stretch and Limber-up

Do the Hand Exercises, Basic and Advanced.

Practise manipulating a block the size and shape of a house brick. Show the shape with your fingers.

Do the Face Exercises.

Practise the four expressions and snap between them.

Do the Voice Exercises.

Look at the Homework.

Don't reveal what each environment is until after it has been performed.

Brainstorm a bit to get more ideas for each of the environments people want to convey. What other ways can you show where you are, economically and entertainingly?

'The two main conditions of the actor's work are improvisation and the power of self-restraint' (Meyerhold).

Do the Feet Exercises.

Practise Climbing Stairs.

Technique: Descending Stairs

This is similar to the climbing stairs technique in Workshop 9.

Your hand pulls the rail from down in front of you, while

you use a rise onto the ball of one foot to enable you to drop onto the other, as if you were stepping down.

The Feet and Legs.

These convey the illusion of stepping down as follows. Lift the right foot up and bring it forward a few inches, leading with the knee. Flex the foot and begin to straighten the knee. As you do so, rise up as tall as you can on the ball of the left foot. Both legs are straight for a moment here. The right foot, being flexed, is a couple of inches off the floor, so you now lean forward and drop on to it, as if you had just stepped down. The back leg bends at the knee and the heel leaves the floor.

Then you can bring the left leg forward, leading with the knee, flex the foot, straighten the leg out as you rise up on the ball of the other foot, and step down on to the straight leg.

The Hands.

Each time you begin the drop on to the forward foot, pull the hand rail up a segment. Start by reaching in front of you, at the level of your hip, and pull it up to the level of your upper ribs, releasing it near your armpit and reaching out again. As before, the rail pull movement is divided up into distinct segments, pausing inbetween for a leg movement, and the shape must be described faithfully by the hand. Divide the hand action up into two segments this time, and keep it very regular and precise.

Be sure to act. Look down and think, 'Down. I'm going down.' Remember to put the accent on the downward drop, and to raise yourself up almost surreptitiously as you are stepping forward.

The *number* of steps you climb, to convey a standard flight of stairs, should probably be between five and eight. Any less than five being easily counted, will look like a very short climb. Any more than eight begins to get tedious for the audience and can slow down the pace of the drama.

To finish, try rehearsing a mime piece of your own choosing with the semi-improvisational method outlined in Chapter 2. Give everyone the same short scene or sequence to work on for ten minutes and then look at the different interpretations. Choose a scene which is short enough to allow attention to be given to blocking, characterisation, agreement on fixed points, etc. It may only be twenty to thirty seconds. Give people a taste of the concentration and careful working-out that is needed to communicate effectively in mime.

PART 3

The Sketches

Performance Licence

In order to perform the sketches in this book, you need to obtain permission in the form of a licence from the copyright-holders. This is common practice with theatrical works, and it holds for amateur as well as professional performances.

In the case of these pieces, the licence is obtainable on payment of a nominal sum of £2. It gives the holder permission to perform any or all of the sketches for a period of ten years. It will be issued in the name of the individual or group intending to present the material, and is not transferable. It covers amateur performances before non-paying audiences only. Professional performances are subject to individual negotiation.

Acknowledgements in any performance should mention author and publisher.

All recording, video, film and television rights are reserved.

The fee may be sent, with a stamped, self-addressed envelope to: *Steps of Faith*, c/o St. Cuthbert's Centre, Peasholme Green, YORK YO1 2PW

Please make cheques payable to *Steps of Faith*.

Thank you for observing professional etiquette with me in this way.

Money received in this way will go to the Direction Mime Trust to support the work of Christians in mime, and in dance in worship.

17
The Chocolate Box

by J. Geoffrey Stevenson

Solo mime. No props.
Approximate timing: six minutes

Outline

The extremely popular piece has been in the repertoire since the begining of my touring work with Graham Kendrick. It is surreal and slightly black in its humour, since it imagines a person so overtaken by greed that he climbs inside a box of chocolates which, inevitably, traps him. When he is rescued, he must make the choice: stay with the box, or leave to thank and follow his Rescuer. As a parable, it speaks of the power of all kinds of sin if we let them overcome us, it declares the presence and power of a Rescuer who can free us, and it reminds us of the choice we have: to serve one Master or the other. Yet as it is a parable, it does not 'cast pearls before swine'. To those who are not 'seeking', it is, perhaps, just a moral tale.

Method

Enter sL.

Notice, stop, inspect 'box', DsL. (See it has been opened before.)

Lift lid, look in, 'Oooh!!' to audience.

Rub hands with glee, peer in and slowly choose first chocolate with right hand.

Look up on key inside lid, pointing with finger of left hand.

Look at chocolate. Put it carefully back.

Choose a second.

Look up what it is. Make a face of disgust. Put it back with slight distaste.

Choose a third. Look it up. 'Ah'.

Place delicately on tongue and close mouth.

Slowly savour and chew (press tongue into cheeks).

See another. Take it with joy.

Stop to look it up.

Satisfied, eat it. Let a quiver of excitement pass through body.

Go for another one, but change mind, stop, lower lid, turn away sR, (Left hand still on box.)

Pause.

Resolve weakens, slowly turn back, lift lid, look in.

Again, check yourself, lower lid, turn away, etc.

Repeat three times, faster and faster.

End with raising and lowering lid as fast as possible five times.

Stop with slapping own hand and breaking away.

Walk away, and walk back. Pretend to 'discover' the box as for the first time. Make face: 'Ah-ha'. Open and close lid with one hand quickly, peeking at them, and then walk on by, feigning indifference.

Turn on heel and repeat from the other side.

This time lift lid while passing and grab a chocolate, lightning fast. Pop into mouth, chew and take three steps to the side and halt.

Slowly turn, chewing laboriously.

With resignation, and much chewing, finish and swallow, ending with look of disgust.

Glance at 'box', shrug 'why not?', open and choose another chocolate.

Look up in key, and pop into mouth. This is a transport of delight, causing arms to move as angel's wings. Rise on toes, begin to topple to side, and come down with a 'bump'.

Return to box, and greedily jam into the mouth six in a row, cheeks bulging.

Swallow with utter ecstasy.

Beat.

Lift lid, remove 'tray', and 'Oooh' as at beginning.

Shovel in a couple of rows of chocolates.

Push sides of box out, go deeper, grabbing handfuls and stuffing them in.

Repeat this, making box even larger.

Place hands on sides of box, swing leg over and climb in.

Furiously cram the chocolates in with both hands, swallowing and slobbering all over.

Freeze suddenly upon realisation that lid has shut and look up. Pause.

Place hands flat up against underside of lid.

Leave hands there, bring head down to face audience.

Shrug, lower hands, and pop in another chocolate from floor.

Again place hands flat up against underside of lid.

Try pushing up this time, but nothing budges.

A little apprehensive now, push harder.

Beginning to panic, push shoulder up to open lid. It doesn't move.

Frightened, push out on sides with hands with enormous but vain effort.

All this frantic activity suddenly ceases as knocking is heard. Look up.

Pause (two seconds).

Knock back a couple of times on the underside of lid.

Close eyes and listen, nodding to indicate the knocks heard in reply – two more.

Then quickly plead – with hands as if praying. Freeze.

(The lid has been released). Push up with hands – it gives – and swing lid up and open. Come to standing.

Feel fresh air, sunshine, freedom, etc. take a deep breath, before remembering Rescuer.

Turn sL, catch sight of him, and hail with left arm.

Thrust other hand forward, to show you want to shake his. But he is walking away.

Wave 'wait!' Motion for him to come back.

Climb out of box. Try to follow, pulling box with Us hand. It won't move.

Pull with both hands, craning neck so as not to lose sight of disappearing Rescuer.

With one hand on box, other hand stretched to Rescuer, look from him to the hand on the box.

Freeze, and realise need to release the box.

Look to hand.

Uncurl fingers slowly.

Look to audience with joy on face.

Withdraw hand, take step to Rescuer.

Freeze.

Blackout.

18

Deck-chairs on the Titanic

by J. Geoffrey Stevenson,
and the St. Michael's Mime Project

A mime for four persons.
Approximate timing: four minutes

This is a parable for the church, and was created for Spring Harvest 1989, whose theme was the same as this title. It is a warning against complacency and petty squabbling when the situation is in fact very serious, as I believe it is for the church, which is so largely ineffective in many affluent Western democracies. It was first performed on the day the Scottish Free Presbyterian church made the headlines for suspending Lord Mackay, one of its elders, for attending two Roman Catholic requiem masses. Enough said.

Outline

The atmosphere of the ocean liner's exciting departure is created with a few props, costumes and sound effects. Life at sea – in luxury class, anyway – is marvellous: promenading on deck, drinking champagne, and stretching out in comfortable deck-chairs. An argument over seating between two passengers assumes fanatical importance – until the crash. The boat starts to go down.

Characters

A & B: could be same sex.
C & D: a couple preferably but could be same sex, one obviously the aged parent.

Requirements

1. Sound-effects of an ocean liner whistle. (Try an effects record, or see what the church organist can do for you.)
2. Sound-effects of an explosion, with ten to twenty second rumble/aftermath. (Try an atomic explosion from a sound-effects record played at a lower speed.)
3. Four ordinary chairs, arranged across the middle of the stage, about half a metre from each other.
4. Period costume would be an advantage, very elegant whites and linens. A collection of about ten extra hats and caps to throw in the air at the beginning would also be good. You could toss up a bunch of rolled-up paper streamers, such as you find in champagne poppers, at the same time.

Method

Blackout

A & B, C & D enter and take up positions: ranged in a line along front of stage, largely to DsL, backs to audience – and freeze.

Fx: one long blast of whistle.

As it ends, all turn and throw hats/streamers straight up in the air, sequencing them if necessary to produce a rain of items. If blackout is available, do this in darkness. Then immediately bring up lights to reveal all waving goodbye with reserved (keep it upper-class) enthusiasm and variety:

blowing kisses, waving with both arms, waving own hat, one with arm around shoulders of companion, etc.

Fx: three short blasts;

On first blast, all begin moving sideways to sR with heel-toe step (described in *Steps of Faith*, p 61).

(It is important to remain locked in relative position to one another, using such aids as keeping whole body stiff, tying in with others through slight touch, such as hands of two people resting on same 'rail', etc. Practise this in pairs – all combinations – first, to get used to rhythm of movement.)

Shortly after setting off, look around in surprise at motion, and redouble the farewells.

(Remember how far away the people on dock would be, and how hard it would be to pick them out in a huge crowd seeing the boat off, and act accordingly. But keep moving smoothly.)

When whistle has died away, stop.

Partners swivel heads in unison with big grins, deliver same 'gaze' (see Workshop 8) to audience, and erupt into joyous leaps, silent cheering, etc. Run to sC and click heels. Turn and do a little Hornpipe step if you know one, and jig around a bit.

All suddenly stop together – look at companion, wherever they are, recover composure and dignity and offer arm, 'Shall we Walk?'

A & B must contrive to 'reassemble' sL, C & D on the opposite side.

They turn in pairs towards sC, pause for a beat, and are about to proceed to pace the deck (begin to take a step), but then stop, each staring in surprise at the other pair.

Trying to get around, A & B and C & D both side-step upstage simultaneously.

Smiling with tight lips, after a beat, they try again, stepping down-stage and dipping the heads slightly, only to be brought up short again by the other couple.

Repeat with mounting impatience, the weaker of each pair glancing at the stronger member who is stubbornly determined (NB: find your character, folks).

At the same time they condescendingly offer to give way to each other, only to come up short in the centre as both pairs take advantage of the offer.

Both couples turn on their heels and begin to walk away. A & B stop first, after a couple of steps, to pick up a hat that has fallen nearby, and one of them gleefully sails it overboard, in a rightish direction. Both watch it fall, with slow arc, into the sea. Then heads follow it as it swiftly floats past towards the 'stern' of the boat, ie towards sL.

They look at one another, chuckle, turn sL and take two paces, then freeze.

C & D meanwhile have stopped, frozen at the far side of the stage. When they hear A & B move off again, they count two beats before coming to life, turning to lean on and over the rail. They are watching the seagulls wheeling and diving over the sea.

Perhaps they make the noise of seagulls – a falsetto 'kee-ow, kee-ow, kee-ow, kee-ow'. (A & B can make the noise from their position, to help.) One of them pulls a small 'paper bag' from pocket, removes and tosses out the bits of a sandwich. The gull noises increase as the bits are tossed out.

When the noise stops, A & B turn and face sC. After one step, they stop and see 'deck-chairs'.

A gestures to B with sweeping arm gesture, 'Would you like a seat?' B nods and accepts, taking the nearest of the middle two seats. A settles him/her, passing behind the chair, placing hands on the back of the chair, head coming round to inquire (just the head gesture, no word spoken or mouthed), 'Everything all right?'

A takes other middle seat. They settle in comfortably. They order and receive champagne from a passing steward, clinking glasses and taking a sip. They freeze.

C & D unfreeze, move toward chairs, only to find middle two occupied. They look behind them at one empty chair, then to the other on the far side of the stage.

Make a 'What now?' shrug to one another.

They turn heads and stare at other couple.

After a beat, A & B coolly turn and meet the stare. C & D both look at A, and then point with their chins to the empty chair beyond. A & B swivel heads to look at it, swivel back to look at C & D, and then turn faces forward. They take a sip of champagne.

Either C or D brings hand to mouth and mimes an attention-grabbing throat clearing.

When A & B look, he/she jerks head towards the chair. Beat. A & B look to C & D, turn heads to look at each other, shrug and turn faces to look front, taking another sip of champagne.

C seats D carefully in the seat behind them (sR) and stands by the chair scowling at A & B who ignore them.

They finish their glasses, and A, with a tilt of the head, inquires of B whether they would like another. Nods, 'Oh yes. Rather!' He attempts to attract 'steward' with snap of fingers, fails two or three times as steward passes in alternate directions. Finally takes B's glass and gets up to follow steward off towards sL. Freeze at edge of stage.

C watches him go, looks at empty chair next to him, looks to partner, 'Why not?' and seizes chair. Takes it to partner's side, puts it down, and settles in.

B does not apparently notice (perhaps he/she is reading, or dozing).

A returns with champagne, sees situation, hands glasses to B, and marches over to C.

He taps her on the shoulder.

She turns head, coolly meets his gaze, and turns head away.

He is uncertain how to react. He marches across the back to

try the other chair on the far sL, but it is in the shade, and anyway, his pride gets the better of him.

He marches back to behind where C is sitting and with a yank, pulls chair out from under her and starts with it back to its original position.

She very nearly falls to the deck, but recovers in time to plant herself halfway on the chair which A is just about to sit on.

It takes a moment for this to sink in before A and C simultaneously leap to their feet, turn and scowl at each other.

A controlled tug of war ensues over the chair, which is briefly interrupted by explosion/crash of collision.

Fx: explosion

On the sound of the explosion A, B, C, and D all throw themselves to the right to show collision. The other two rise in panic and exit behind A and C, B perhaps helping the frail D to safety (all struggle to keep balance).

A and C continue their tug of war, gradually sinking lower and lower until they are on their knees.

After an agreed number of pulls, the explosion suddenly ceases. A and C freeze, pause for a beat, and then snap heads to audience with expression of horror on their faces.

Freeze.

Blackout.

19

Dreaming

(I am indebted to Julie and Robert Jack for the idea and first performance of this piece)

Mime duet. No props
Approximate timing: two minutes

Outline

Dreaming is a simple story of a girl who dreams of a romantic lover, of his arrival and of how he will woo her and sweep her off her feet. She is awakened by a knock on the door. It is her boyfriend, who treats her very differently. He only wants one thing, and when she refuses, he strikes her and storms out. Alone again, face in her hands, she cries.

Dreaming is perhaps useful as a discussion starter or illustration in the area of boy/girl relationships. There are no great value judgements here, just a picture of the all-too-common gulf that divides the sexes.

The piece may be played in modern dress, with or without white face. Please note and observe the mime convention of not touching during the embraces, etc. Always maintain a gap: it may be difficult to achieve, but it will enhance the dramatic moments a great deal. Also, do not rush these moments. If it is wished, music may be played in the background (something slushy and romantic), fading out when the boyfriend enters and fading back in again as she sobs at the end. The dream/fantasy may be elaborated upon at the discretion of the performer. The girl is wistful and all too willing to lapse into dreaming. The boyfriend should be played brusque and severe, but not bullying or leering. Underplay, if in doubt.

Method

Girl (G) enters from sL to Centre. Faces front.

As she passes, she catches sight of herself in a mirror a few feet to the right of Centre, on the fourth wall – that is, the audience. She goes back to it, makes some minor adjustment to her hair, looks at her reflection and sighs. She is not very encouraged by what she sees.

She steps back, and looks somewhat dejectedly around the room to check that everything is tidy. (It isn't very neat, but she can't be bothered.) She steps to a 'window' a few feet to the left of Centre (again, facing the audience), draws back a 'curtain', and looks up and down the street. She gives her watch a quick glance. Pause. She sighs (silently).

She takes a couple of steps upstage and turns around to sit in an imaginary chair, facing downstage. She rests chin on hand and same elbow on back of other hand, and settles down to doze. See illustration overleaf.

As soon as her eyes close, she does a rising turn, opening her eyes on the way around, with hands held out to the side slightly. This is to convey that what happens next is in her dream.

When turn is complete she is pleased and surprised, looking to edge of sR at 'door', as if she had just heard the knock of her long awaited lover. She crosses to it, opens it, and with love in her eyes steps back to watch entrance of 'her man' (entirely imaginary). She follows this dream figure with her

eyes and head, gazing at him as he crosses in front of her to DsL.

She gasps (silently) as she sees large bouquet of flowers appear from behind his back. She takes them, beaming, and smells them deeply, passing them before her face.

Adjusting her hold of them she selects a flower and puts

it into her hair, above one ear. Then another, above other ear.

She smells bouquet again (not necessary to the mime piece, just pleasurable for the character!), turns, and places them down somewhere upstage.

(Don't walk through the chair – the audience may still be imagining it where you were sitting.)

She turns front again.

Pause, as she looks invitingly (but not wantonly) at 'her man'. She opens her arms, lifting them to shoulder height, reaches for shoulders of her lover as she imagines she is taken around her waist by his arms. At the same time she begins to turn. When she finishes, back to audience, her hands are wrapped around her, and she is being caressed by her own hands, on shoulder and waist. (It's the old cliché – don't overdo it.)

By lifting her shoulders and tilting her head, she presses her cheek to the hand on her shoulder, twice, before resting her head on the hand with a sense of peace and blissful protection, etc.

Short pause, then she turns a half turn and 'flows' into her original dream position, closing her eyes and settling down again, still asleep. She gives a (silent) sigh in her sleep as a dreamy smile passes across her face.

Pause.

Boyfriend (B) enters sR, knocks on 'door' (stamp foot for knocking fx). G starts, open-mouthed, and looks toward door, then to her watch (what has happened to the time?). She raises hands, 'Oh dear!' and rises. She steps to door, pulls it open, and welcomes boyfriend with glad expression on her face, stepping back as he enters.

B strides in and across the room, nearly brushing her aside. He turns and faces her sL. She looks at him expectantly as he enters, hoping for a tender romantic greeting. But he only rocks back on his heels, and stares at her, perhaps even motioning for her to shut the door. A little deflated, she does so.

She turns to him, and leans forward slightly to be kissed, closing her eyes. After a second's pause he rushes upon her, in a fierce embrace that pushes her back two steps. She leans back from the the waist as his arms encircle her.

(NB: the performers are to do this without touching. Imagine you are embracing someone who is two centimetres larger all round.)

He would kiss her, but she turns her head violently away to each side, and then brings her arms up in front of her to push him away.

She pushes hard (without touching) and, releasing her, he falls back.

Surprised but not deterred (he thinks she is perhaps playing hard-to-get), he lunges in again, but her hands come up and he stops. He grabs her shoulder with upstage hand, but she twists away, turning her back to him. (However, she looks back at him, so she can react to his blow.)

He strikes her with the back of his hand. He is then at a loss what to do, momentarily. She recoils from the blow (as his hand passes her face she goes with the blow). She puts her hand to her mouth, devastated, and stares at him like a frightened rabbit.

Pause.

He sweeps her out of his way. (This time let his hand touch her upper arm, as a signal to her that she is to be pushed aside.)

The boyfriend pulls open the door and storms out, slamming it behind him. Exit sR.

Make sure the handle he takes is the same type as she used earlier.

The girl looks up sharply, as at the sound of the door closing, looks around slowly, walks aimlessly to sC.

She covers her face with her hands and begins sobbing gently. She sinks to her knees, head in hands, still sobbing.

Take time over this last sequence, from when B exits, at least twenty seconds.

Ends.

20
The Good News is Like . . .

Solo mime. No props.
Approximate timing: four minutes

Outline

This very simple mime parable originated as an exercise at a Paris mime school with the following instructions:

> Establish an ironing board, take something and begin to iron it. You are in a particular mood. The phone rings, you answer it – and whatever you hear completely changes your mood. Return to the ironing showing this new attitude.

My character started out depressed and ended up overjoyed. It struck me later that, with very little added, this was a parable about the effect the gospel has on our lives. If it doesn't make a difference to the way we do things here and now, how can it be such good news?

Of course I'm not suggesting that the gospel magically turns a hopeless and dreary situation into an experience of ecstasy –

the sketch is a parable. It depends on a context of teaching and explanation for it to make its point. Clearly understood, it may be a spur to praise and celebration.

I am indebted to Martin Thompson for the alternative ending in which the hearer of good news cannot refrain from getting back on the phone and passing it on. In this case a very important point is made, namely, how natural it should be to share something that has given us great joy (see the parable of the cancelled debts, Lk 7: 41–3).

Method

Enter, shoulders drooping, face glum, to sC. Pause – look at audience.

Raise and then collapse head and chest to indicate a (silent) sigh.

Place hands flat on 'ironing board' in front of you.

Look at 'iron' to your right (or left, if you iron left-handed).

Take it, pick it up, touch middle finger of other hand to tongue, then bring it to sole plate of 'iron' to test heat (optional fx: sharp hiss). Jerk hand away smartly.

Show face to audience – with expression even darker.

Put down iron.

Reach down to one side and pick up a 'towel' from pile of laundry, first with thumb and forefinger of one hand, then take other corner with other hand. Hold it up very briefly to look at it, swing it over the board like a table cloth, release it.

With hands perfectly flat, and in two spreading movements, smooth it out.

Place one hand down on board, pick up iron with other. Pause a moment, look to audience, and sigh deeply, as before.

Place iron down, and iron: back and forth, back and forth, forward and back, forward and back.

Lift iron to check towel. React, 'What, still wrinkled?'

Iron harder, pressing down with both hands on handle.

Finish, replace iron (standing up) to the side.

Pick up far corners of towel, fold them towards you, pick up side corners, fold it across. Smooth it, pick it up, put it down on a 'table' behind you.

Turn back to audience. Sigh.

Reach down for another towel.

Begin to repeat towel ironing sequence exactly as before, up until second pass across with iron.

Stop, hearing phone ring.

(The iron is face down.)

Lift head up to audience, then across sL to look at phone.

Take a step towards the phone, and be sure not to look at iron as you move towards phone.

Leave hand with iron in it behind until arm is nearly straight, then release it (thereby showing that iron is still on towel) and proceed another step or two to the phone.

Answer it, with irritation clearly expressed.

Do not mouth any words, but show through nods, frowns, etc. what your character's replies are:

'Yes. What is it?'

'Yes, that's me.'

'What?'

'You're not serious.'

'You *are*?'

(During this whole 'conversation' be careful not to look toward your ironing board.)

'I've won *how* much?' (or whatever is going to excite your character the most).

Give small, exultant cheer with arms, quickly returning to mouthpiece:

'Really?'

Give a bigger cheer, but doubt brings you back again:

'Really?'

An even bigger cheer, and back to phone:

'*Really*?'

Leap into the air with the next cheer, then toss phone up with one hand, catch the cord and swing it around in a big circle a couple of times.

Catch it, wave goodbye into mouthpiece, and saunter back to ironing, tremendously pleased.

Freeze at sight of smoke rising from ironing board. Lunge towards it, and with some effort lift iron up and put it in its place.

Look at ruined towel, raise arms in fury – as if about to utter an oath – suddenly stop, remembering the good news.

Look to the phone, back to the towel, look to audience, relax hands and arms and turn it into a shrug to say, 'No problem, Eh?'

Pick up towel by far corners.

Pull it to face and look through the 'hole' in it.

Change grip and thrust arm through, wiggling fingers, making a big joke out of it.

Crumple it up, look to phone briefly, and then toss the towel high into the air.

Freeze with arm stretched up, head up, and great joy on the face.

Alternative ending

After throwing the towel up in the air, rush back to the phone and ring a friend, excitedly sharing your good news with them. Freeze with one hand in the middle of a small cheer, face in a grin.

21
The History of Music

Sketch for Solo Mime. No props.
Approximate timing: four minutes.
Suggested use: street theatre, youth club, evangelistic programme.

Outline

The History of Music consists of five scenes humorously tracing the development in personal musical entertainment: transistor radio; a small cassette player (single speaker); a larger box, still held up to the side of the head; an enormous ghetto-blaster, almost too heavy to lift; and lastly, a tiny Walkman-type personal stereo with headphones.

The character is seen grooving appropriately to each, the beat and volume of the music heard is indicated by the nodding of the head. In a surreal and black ending, the agonising noise cannot be got rid of – not even by throwing away the stereo and ripping off the headphones. The character clutches his head wildly as the 'beat goes on'.

As a parable, this represents much of what our culture provides. Leisure, comfort, transport and entertainment are all things that can seem harmless enough. Indeed they are all good in their way, but any of them can take us over in the end. They get inside our head, dictate our way of thinking, and we can't hear the still small voice of the Lord.

Side exits, such as screens on either side of the performing area, where the mime can completely disappear, are the ideal. Next best would be a screen UsC, from either side of which he can appear. There is much humour in this, which is heightened enormously by a lightning quick turn and re-appearance almost immediately each time the character exits.

Method

Enter from sR, eyes closed, snapping fingers, right hand holding a 'transistor radio' to ear. (Possible tune to imagine: 'Twist and Shout').

(Be sure fingers really describe this small rectangular shape.)

Cross stage, and half way across begin in your enthusiasm to do 'The Twist' as you walk, but quickly (after two–three twists) bring radio back to ear because you can't hear music.

Exit, still snapping fingers of left hand. (10 to 12 seconds)

Immediately reappear, going back across stage with a somewhat larger box pressed to your right ear, and held with both hands.

(Show shape with right angles in hands.)

Music is, perhaps, 'Lucy in the sky with diamonds'.

Take hand away once for a slower snapping of fingers, all the time with a dazed, far-out look on the face. The posture and walk have changed to a hippy slouch. Just before the exit, turn face to audience, and mouth, 'Oh *Wow*' with very clear lip movements. (15 to 18 seconds)

Immediately re-enter, both hands holding a large cassette player that appears to be at least 30 inches long and 8 inches wide. Head is moving up and down to the beat quite sharply.

Occasionally head vibrates rather violently sideways away from the speakers to a heavy passage in the music – which is probably Pink Floyd or Led Zeppelin. The right arm comes down to try to snap fingers in time to music, but must return after a couple of snaps because of the enormous weight of the box, which when not supported by both hands, causes right side of body to collapse a bit, with staggering and apparent risk of falling. Exit (ear drums bloody).

(12 to 15 seconds)

A beat, then re-enter from sL, both arms stretched absolutely vertically downwards, carrying by the handle a huge stereo cassette music centre, just managing to hold this enormous weight off the ground while staggering forward.

Box is held to the left or downstage side, requiring upper half of body to lean towards audience, while legs and feet continue walk towards side.

Hold head up, determined to move forward, and every few steps, lower box to floor, release right hand and, with deadpan stare at audience, snap fingers twice in time to music (reggae) before resuming the slow progress.

When halfway across stage, suddenly stop, in mid-finger-snap, as attention is caught and all movement arrested by an extraordinary sight passing from your right to left. This should be about where the middle of the audience is.

(Try to see it very clearly so that the eyes, including the way they focus, follow this sight. The head may also make a very slight and rapid nod about once a second, to indicate that it is a person walking. This must be separated by a pause from any previous head-nodding to the music, and must also be qualitatively different. If in doubt, leave it out.)

Watch character reach, as it were, extreme edge of audience area, then bring head front with a blank expression on the face.

Look down at 'music centre', look back towards the person with the tiny personal stereo, and again down to own bulky system, look to audience and scowl.

Look down again, look straight up to sky where you have just determined to throw your now completely obsolete equipment.

Look at system once more as you grasp handle carefully with each hand.

Bend knees and assume an ape-like expression.

Remembering its enormous weight, lift it off the ground as

a weight-lifter, and straining hard, begin to swing it back and forth, a little higher each time.

At the end of the fifth swing, with a superhuman effort, propel this thing straight up into the air and watch it as it climbs.

(Imagine it turning over and over, and convey these rotations with a circling of the head – the circle is in a vertical plane – that slows down as the machine reaches the height of its trajectory. Imagine it fifty feet up.)

There is a slight pause, and then a look of astonishment comes over your (now prehistoric man) face.

Sink to your knees. The object is being transformed (echoing a scene from '2001: Space Odyssey').

It begins to rotate again as it falls to earth, faster and faster.

Just in time, put out your hands to catch this strange new object.

A brief pause as you stare at it.

Stand up, still staring.

Scratch head in bewilderment, but as you lift your hand something drops and is now dangling from the object.

Reach down and take hold of it between thumb and forefinger (it is the lightweight headphones).

Look at it and then back to the object, eyes following the cord that connects them.

Look the object over, and with a flash of inspiration that is completely out of character, see on it a hook that enables you to hang it on your belt. Do this, enabling you to examine the headphones.

Shift your grip to the two earpieces and then test the springiness by pulling them a little further apart.

The third time you hold them apart, and surprising no-one as much as yourself, lift them to your head and release them over your ears.

(One beat for this to sink in.)

Follow the cord hand over hand (about four times) back down to the player, then unhook it and hold it in your left hand, examining the topside of it very closely.

With right index finger approach the sparkling and confusing buttons, pause for a beat and then stab at one.

Pause for a beat, then suddenly head indicates flashy, jumpy music by nodding and jerking (about four or five per second for four seconds).

A look of alarm fills the face. Stab in panic at the player – immediately your head stops dead – followed after a beat by a huge grin which slowly spreads across the face as if to say, 'Oooh, that was good.!' (Be sure to show this to the audience.)

Look down and stab at it again, head jerking and nodding as before, quite fast.

Enjoy it now – snap fingers a couple of times, really getting into it.

Then 'see' something else – a slider. Push with the thumb of right hand – it is the volume control. Immediately all head movements dramatically increase in size (same rhythm).

In alarm turn it down again – this time make head movements to same pattern and rhythm, but very small and contained.

Continuing with this head waggle, look down, and then push another button.

Noise (and therefore head) stops, followed closely by a pulling back of the head in alarm to indicate that the lid has popped open.

Take hold of (be very careful to form fingers in the correct shape) and remove the cassette from the player, holding it by the side edges and drawing it away and up in a straight line for a good twelve inches before examining it, both sides.

Twist hand through 180° to flip cassette over and re-insert it, other side up.

Release, then press lid down. Press the play button again.

Pause. Look front.

Look left and right with just the eyes. Beat.

You are just about to look down in puzzlement when music begins. Head is violently jerked up and down, more slowly than before, about two beats per second (chin down and up again is about one beat).

Show delight on face, turn volume up (head moves even more violently) and replace player at waist.

Groove to this for a few seconds, then turn head in profile, bring hand to mouth to cover yawns – two in quick succession.

Remove player from belt, holding it in left hand, and punch off-button (head jerking all the time). Noise doesn't stop.

Punch it again. Still it goes on.

Rapidly stab at two buttons alternately about six times.

Slam the top of it with fist a couple of times.

(If you have trouble keeping the head movement going during this, don't worry – just be sure the beat is very obvious during the pauses between the actions.)

Grab the headphone lead just below the chin, follow it back down to the player.

Take hold of the plug and, after a beat, jerk it clear.

Head still banging, look in bafflement from the player in one hand to the plug two feet away in the other.

Reinsert and jerk it out again a couple of times.

Fear comes over the face.

Throw the player away to the left, and stare at the plug, head still jerking.

Hands climb the lead up to your neck and then grasp the phones beside each ear. They seem to be glued there, and it is with difficulty that you eventually wrench them off and throw them away.

Head is still for two beats – no more – and then it starts again.

Face fills with terror, hands go to cover ears, elbow high – the head nod now becomes a convulsive jerk that lifts the whole body off the ground.

Jump five times and freeze – show face up and out to audience in a mask of fear.

Blackout if possible. Otherwise hold freeze for at least four seconds (count them out) before relaxing and sprinting off stage.

22
The Addicts

Mime duet without props.
Approximate timing: six minutes, forty seconds

Outline

In this mime, a dramatic parallel is drawn between psychological addiction and frantic, careless driving. The addictions are several: heroin, glue, social drinking, vanity and chocolate. They are each played out seriously but in a matter-of-fact way, without melodrama, alternating with the noisy and increasingly manic driving that leads to a crash at the end.

This mime was devised for a Youth for Christ European programme that itself was devised for the International Year of the Young Person in 1985. It is a simple morality piece. Some might call it simplistic. To lump together heroin addiction and a craving for chocolate, glue sniffing and vanity, and to ascribe guilt rather than offer excuses offends in our prevailing humanist culture.

However, the spiritual destruction at the end of a life beset by all such sin requires a warning. At the same time, it is up to individual Christians not to judge and condemn those they deal with who are trapped in destructive lifestyles. On a personal level, understanding and compassion are needed.

The mime should therefore be presented in a context where such issues can be opened up and discussed, rather than as incontrovertible argument.

The addict (*B*) may be male or female. The driver is better if male, owing to the machismo usually associated with reckless driving, and the need for very loud and aggressive sound-effects.

On stage the mimes are separate, but they must work together closely to ensure smooth and rapid transitions between each other's sequences. The sound-effects (fx) of the driver (*A*) are made by the mime himself – it can be quite funny. The addictions are played in silence. The driver and addict must be positioned so that the driver can see the other out of the corner of his eye. The addict needn't be able to see the driver, but can react to sound cues.

Method.

B is just left of sC and facing upstage.

1A

A enters from sR, unlocks and opens 'car door', climbs in and sits to Right of sC (real chair may be used).

Removes 'key' from pocket and places it in ignition.

Pulls seat belt across chest and clicks it in.

Wiggles 'gear lever' to ensure that it is out of gear, places one hand on 'wheel' and switches on ignition.

Places foot on accelerator and pumps it, then turns key further to fire starter motor.

After two or three tries, it fires. Revs it.

Shifts into first gear, places both hands on wheel and accelerates, (fx) just before change into second. Freeze.

1B

B turns around.

Roll up 'sleeve' well past elbow. Unbuckle 'belt', pull it out of trousers.

Lay it across 'bare' upper arm, wrap it round and pull it tight. Take hold of syringe and needle from a 'ledge' in front of him, clench fist of 'bare' arm, find vein and jab with needle.

Press syringe.

Pause for two counts.

Lift head to show audience appropriate expression (not exaggerated).

Freeze for three seconds, then turn round when *A* comes in (fx). Freeze.

2A

A changes up into second gear. Steers hard, left turn then hard right turn. Accelerates (fx) and changes up into third (fx). Freeze.

2B

B faces audience.

Unzip 'jacket' and remove folded paper bag from inner pocket.

Unfold several times.

Take hold of near edges and shake open once or twice.

Put it down on imagined ledge in front, reach into side pocket for glue.

Hold it up, regard it for a moment, then take top with other hand and unscrew.

Discard.

Take up bag, plunge hand with 'glue' into it and squeeze tube.

Repeat and, putting bag down for a moment, squeeze out tube into bag with both hands.

Discard tube into bag, take bag with both hands, draw up to level of mouth.

Short pause.

Breathe out (silently) and pulling hands up to side of face, breathe in. Change grip with one hand supporting bottom of bag, breathe deeply again. Freeze for three seconds, then turn round and freeze.

3A

A completes shift into third. Acceleration. (fx). Steer hard right turn, straighten up (tyre squeal fx). Down shift with much revving (fx) into second. Freeze, and cut.

3B

B turns round, roaring with laughter, 'glass' in one hand, and with other hand gesticulating and generally assisting animated party conversation.

Alternate this with three sips from drink, leaving 'glass' empty.

Break off conversation to reply to offer of another drink – 'What? Oh yes, thank you very much' with eyebrows and nodding.

Hold out glass, while indicating with other hand 'only a little one'.

Attention returns briefly to conversation while glass is filled – to the brim – and then with quick widening of the eyes and little lick of the lips, takes a sip, and then another.

'Talk' more animatedly, freeze in mid-laugh, pause three seconds (for *A* to begin again).

Slowly turn and face upstage.

4A

A revs engine in second (fx). Wild steering, tyres squeal. (fx). Shifts into third, accelerating (fx). Shifts into fourth (fx). Cut (fx) and freeze.

4B

B turns round, combing or brushing hair. Finish this looking in mirror where the audience is.

Place comb on 'table' and take up bottle of cologne, twisting cap off and putting it down, looking at reflection all the while.

Splash some cologne on and replace cap.

Suddenly, with great dismay notice a small spot.

Stare at it with a frown, before leaning forward and carefully squeezing it. The 'pop' is indicated with a tiny but sharp jerk of the elbows.

Satisfied, wipe the area with finger tips.

Turn to one side, pull open a 'wardrobe door', and select a 'garment'.

Hold it against body to check it in a mirror, but decide against it – the colour is not right.

Lay it on a chair and select another. Reject that one quickly.

Similarly take out a third and hold it up, before eventually settling on the first one. Admire self from several angles as you slip it on. (If male, do this while buttoning the shirt, tucking it in and adjusting the collar and cuffs according to fashion.)

Finish by making a 'kiss' to self in the mirror.

Freeze.

5A

A is still accelerating (fx) and steering wildly. He shifts down to third, steers round sharp corner, squeal of tyre (fx) and accelerates, shifting back into fourth, (fx). Cut (fx) and freeze.

5B

B turns round and discovers box of chocolates in front of him. Extremely pleased, open box and fold back lid with hands. Delighted expression, hands up and fingers twitching in anticipation. Select one chocolate, place it on tongue, close mouth around and chew. Eyes closed, an expression of serene bliss comes over face.

Swallow.

Eyes open, then light on another favourite chocolate.

Glance guiltily left, then right, then carefully pick it out of the box. Closing eyes, pop it into mouth. There is a moment of stillness as it dissolves on tongue and flavour hits taste buds. Smile, then a shudder of delight passes through body.

Recover, chew blissfully, swallow, and make to close lid. Instead, see another 'favourite'. Hesitate.

Close lid resolutely, leaving hands on box. Look away, but sneak a look back.

Slowly open lid, hesitate, then courageously slowly close it. Open, then close, open, close – faster and faster, ten times – suddenly stop, pop a chocolate into mouth and freeze, with mouth full.

Pause three seconds for *A* to begin again, slowly turn and face upstage.

A accelerates, then tyres screech as steering wheel turns uselessly in his hands. Screech continues as he raises arms in slow motion in front of face.

Meanwhile *B* goes through each of the five finishing poses very smartly in quick succession, holding each one for no longer than two seconds.

End with a pose identical to *A*, arms up in front of face trying to protect himself at the last minute, crash imminent. Freeze/Blackout

(Optional: both make noise of crash/explosion.)

The piece ends with silence – driver stops screech (fx) one short beat after addict raises arms.

Both mimes should aim to stiffen arms and upper bodies into their final freeze at the same moment the sound-effects stop.

Hold the freeze for at least four seconds before relaxing and moving off stage.

23

Kitchen Sink

by J. Geoffrey Stevenson and Conway Barker

Mime duet. No props.
Approximate timing: six minutes, thirty seconds

Outline

This mime is a simple and amusing depiction of tension and lack of communication between family members Martha and Mary, except that the 'one thing' Mary has chosen is a personal stereo – to the extreme annoyance of Martha. (The two could also be a parent and teenage son or daughter.) The mime may be useful as a visual aid or discussion starter on the subject of family tensions.

Requirements

Sound effects are to be made by the performers themselves. The tinny percussion that escapes from a personal stereo someone else is using should accompany the nodding of the head in time to the 'music'. It should be made as loudly as possible without moving the lips, but with the tongue on the roof of the mouth: tschhh – tschhh – tschhh, etc. Performers also make sound-effects of cups crashing to ground at the end.

Costume is at the performers' own discretion. The parent could wear an apron; the son or daughter could be punk in dress and/or hairstyle, or anything outrageous such as luminous pink socks and dyed hair.

Music over the opening mime sequence would be good – anything from a TV 'soap' to suggest domesticity with a melodramatic seriousness.

Method

'A' is the parent.

'B' is the teenage son or daughter.

A is scraping plates, facing audience. She places pile of plates into basin in front of her, turns on taps, and briefly rinses pile under taps.

She stops, watching water, which is not running away.

She puts plates on side, turns off taps, and tries to clear 'bits' away from drain. One hand finally finds plug-hole and grasps small amount of debris, pulls it up and puts it in other hand, cupped.

Two more 'fingers-full' are removed.

Continues with sound-effects and head nodding. Finally picks up 'glass' and tea-towel and uses one on the other.

A stops washing up, finishing a cup, and reaches up and over – turns down 'stereo'.

(fx: music down, but not off.)

B stops, looks at A, who returns to her washing and finishes drying glass.

He reaches up to 'stereo' and turns it back up.

(fx: music up.)

B starts drying 'cup'.

A stops, looks at stereo. Looks at B.

A finishes washing another cup, reaches up and pushes 'stop button' on stereo.

(fx: music stops)

B stops, shoots a sharp look at A, looks at stereo, looks at A, finishes drying cup and defiantly switches stereo on again.

(fx: music as before.)

A stops, slow look at B (she is losing patience now), slow look at stereo, finishes washing 'plate', puts down brush, wipes hands on apron reaches across to pick up stereo and with other hand unplugs B's earphones.

B stops, A gives him plug and places stereo on shelf in front of her, out of B's reach. She returns to washing.

B looks at plug in his hand, looks at A (he can't quite believe it), and looks at each again in turn, before letting plug drop down.

He pauses a moment, then reaches for his stereo, but A has a washed cup ready to place in his hand before it can get there.

B takes it, chagrined. He dries it.

They wash and dry another two items.

B watches A for an opportune moment to try again.

He lunges for the stereo, but so does A, who gets it first.

B knocks her hand, both hands freeze and heads follow stereo as it drops into washing-up.

A reacts first, fishing it out and brushing off 'suds'. A is apologetic. B is stunned. He accepts back the stereo and slowly picks up his headphone jack and plugs it in.

He pushes play button. Result: music that sloshes (fx).

Stop.

Start (same fx). (His anger mounts). Stop.

He slowly places stereo back on shelf in front of him. He removes headphones and places them on top of stereo.

While A looks on, he carefully selects a fine china cup with his left hand, takes it delicately by the handle in his right, little finger extended, turns slightly towards A, holds cup aloft and opens his hand.

A dives and catches 'cup' six inches off the floor.

B is disappointed, but quickly selects another cup and drops it in the same way.

A catches it in her other hand. Both hands are full.

B is surprised but not deterred. In fact, he is triumphant as he picks up a third cup, and, stepping back, tosses it so that its trajectory takes it right in front of where A is by this time kneeling.

Both A and B watch it approach A, who, amazingly is able to begin juggling all three cups.

B watches with amazement for a moment, then calmly and deliberately picks up a long-stemmed 'wine glass' admires it briefly, and holds it out.

A watches in horror, then shakes her head: 'no, no, *no*'

She stops juggling.

Heads of A and B together watch three cups go up and smash to the ground in even succession.

B expresses mock innocence as he picks up towel and carefully dries the 'glass' he still has, holding it up to the light to check it is sparkling clean and dry. He places it carefully (very carefully) down, takes towel in both hands between thumb and forefingers and drapes it over A's head, still kneeling on the floor. He exits calmly sL.

A removes towel from head, stands, and slaps it into one hand in anger.

Freeze.

Blackout.

24
Unemployment

Solo mime. No props.
Approximate timing: five minutes.

Outline

Illusionary pantomime in which one character is seen in a sequence of six episodes: waiting; signing on for unemployment benefit; checking job ads in newspaper; going for (fruitless) interview; playing arcade video game; expressing all the built-up frustration and rage in violence.

There is no obvious message to this mime – it is just a slice-of-life piece, designed to indicate that whatever the causes of long-term unemployment, the effect is evil and dehumanising. Our response starts with understanding and compassion.

The piece may be played in silence, with the mime artist himself making only the noises of the space invaders' game. It can be played against a background of driving rock or heavy-metal music (*not* loud), or (particularly if performed for video or television) with appropriate background sound effects for each episode such as busy office noise, street noise traffic, sedate or muted office noise, as in plush company offices, video arcade noises, and street noise again.

Requirements

White-face is recommended to stylise character, but the decision is left to the performer. He also decides about the costume, but note – 'realism' should not mean that the costume masks the body's movements and gestures. A suggestion: jeans and a sweatshirt with the sleeves cut off. If the performer dresses in costume as a 'mime', he should avoid anything that is too 'pretty', too 'flash' or too clown-like.

Method

Character (or 'C') enters UsL. Faces audience.

Looks right (sees 'queue of people'), looks centre (blank expression), looks left, registers 'shelf'.

He takes two steps to it, places elbow on it (imagine the kind of form-filling-in stations at elbow height in public offices) and leans on it (very casual).

He looks right, looks centre (bored expression).

Then eyes (only) dart up and see 'fly' buzzing lazily.

He follows it with his eyes (just his eyes!), back and forth, back and forth, two loop-the-loops. It then lands on his left hand, he glances at it and flicks it away.

Pause. Gives a silent sigh.

He looks right (decides to join queue), takes two or three steps across to sL of Centre.

Crosses arms, looks out to audience (still bored), gives silent sigh.

He moves with the queue thus: one step forward, bring feet together, wait.

Cross arms, or 'sigh', or peer over shoulder of fellow in front. (Resigned expression – no hurry, he has all the time in the world.) Repeat three times, turning 'corner' to face downstage, just sR of Centre. He reaches 'window' and (according to local practice) signs on (pen doesn't work, at first) for benefit.

(If this is not your local practice, then choose a simple bureaucratic activity characteristic of the state's registration or recognition of the unemployed.)

C turns sL, small wave 'see you again, man' and walks (*marche-sur-place*, in profile).

Stops after three steps.

Sees newsvendor, holds finger up for one paper, reaches into downstage 'pocket', extracts 'coin', exchanges for 'paper', receiving (folded) paper with same hand.

He unfolds it, snaps it straight, to look at front page. Opens paper.

He glances through several pages, then quickly turns on to job ads.

He folds paper inside out, and again in half to go down the list of vacancies.

Runs finger across one notice, pause, looks up. Shakes head, 'No.'

Repeat this, and again with incredulous expression: 'Me? Clean toilets? You must be joking!'

On fourth one, he double-takes after shaking head, considers it again. He looks up pensively, for a second: 'Hmmm. Perhaps.'

Checks notice for time, looks at watch, checks (more urgently) for place, looks up, starts walking (*marche-sur-place, en face*) down-stage, then turns sR, walks (profile) until arriving at correct address, which he checks once more in 'paper' under his arm.

He smooths hair and clothes, pulls open huge door of corporate headquarters, and steps in.

He is in awe of surroundings, but smiles at 'secretary' DsC, presents himself, follows her point to 'personnel director' who is DsR.

Seeing this intimidating individual, his smile drops, he nods 'thanks' to 'secretary' and crosses three steps to DsR.

He bows ever so slightly, is invited to sit, and does so.

(To sit, bend knees slightly keeping back upright, and bring arms to stop on 'chair arms'. Hold that position.)

Place newspaper on 'table' to sR.

Respectful but affable, he corrects spelling of his name, jabbing index towards paperwork.

He smiles and nods 'yes' to several questions: 'No problem', 'Of course I can', 'Oh yes, all the time', etc.

The 'yes' nods then get smaller and are accompanied by an increasing frown. Then a tiny 'no', a bigger 'no', several more embarrassed 'no's and shakes of head.

A desperate and quick smiled 'yes' immediately overtaken by a 'no'. Several more with hands gesturing helplessness, and hiding face.

He stops.

He looks up.

He nods 'yes' (the interview is over).

He rises, turns away sL disappointed.

He is addressed, turns back, shakes hands, turns away. Stops.

He is called back for his paper. He turns and sidles past 'chair' to pick up his 'paper'.

He nods deferentially, and walks (*marche-sur-place*, profile) past 'secretary'. Smiles ruefully, gives thumbs down.

He walks on three paces, stops, then throws away paper into 'bin' downstage, disgustedly.

C walks on three or four more paces, sees 'Space Invader game' DsL. Draws level with it.

Establish location by grasping each side briefly at elbow height, before digging into right pocket for change.

Extracts 'coin' from pocket, places into 'slot' at knee height, presses 'one-player button' takes up position over fire and left/right buttons.

Pause.

Then head translates from side to side as 'left/right buttons' are pushed.

Head appears to slide from side to side, parallel to the ground. Keep rest of body still.

Fx of missiles, repeated pushing of 'fire button'.

Alternate firing with depiction of 'Invaders' on screen in front of face, using hands and fingers – several times, increasing pace.

'Explosion' sends C up and away, wheeling around, hands in air, full circle and immediately returning to playing position.

He stabs at it a couple of times, but the machine is dead.

He kicks it.

He digs for more money, takes out 'coin' (his last).

He hesitates, looks from coin to machine and back to coin in his hand.

He flips coin in the air, watching it up and back down, catches it and slaps it onto back of other hand (heads – I play again, tails – I don't).

It is tails. Disappointment.

Moment of indecision, shrugs 'why not?', flips coin again.

Again, it is tails.

Scowls.

Flips again. Tails again: mounting anger and disbelief.

Flips again and again, faster and faster. It is tails each time.

Then the coin doesn't come down. It has disappeared.

C looks skyward.

If audience laugh, fix them with glare: 'Who are you laughing at? It's all right for you, you've got plenty, but me . . .'

Check pockets – Nothing. Looks down, noticing 'brick'.

Looks left and then right 'Any police?'

Picks up brick, scowls at audience, winds up to throw, face full of hatred.

Freeze.

Blackout.

25
Behold Your God

(Words from Isaiah 40, arranged by Paul Burbridge)

Solo Mime to narration. No props.
Approximate timing: four minutes, thirty seconds.

Outline

For this and the following piece *The Heavenly City*, little or no choreography is given. This is because I believe that there are certain performance qualities that cannot be taught in a book. The words of Scripture here are very moving, however, and the simplest mime can be most effective. But it must be created and acted according to the experience and abilities of the performer. Movements of your own which occur to you while rehearsing will therefore probably be the best.

A few ideas of the mime I perform to this are given to get you started.

Narrator

Have you not known?
Have you not heard?
The Lord is an everlasting God,
Creator of the ends of the earth.

Lift up your eyes on high and see:
Who created these?
It is he who brings out their host by number,
calling them by name.
By the greatness of his might,
and because he is strong in power,
not one is missing.

Enter, react in surprise to Narrator's question. Look around and 'see' the wonders of creation. Finally see the stars in the heavens. Receive and unroll a chart, and try to locate a few constellations in the sky. Surprise that one seems to be missing, but with telescope handed to you, see it and sheepishly tick it off on the chart. Collapse telescope.

God sits above the circle of the earth.
Its inhabitants are like grasshoppers.
He brings princes to nought,
and the rulers of the earth to nothing.
Behold the nations
are as a drop from a bucket,
and are accounted as the dust on the scales.
He stretches out the heavens like a curtain
and spreads them like a tent to dwell in.
He takes up the islands like fine dust.
Every nation is as nothing before him . . .
less than nothing, and emptiness.

Become the Creator, moulding a sphere in the hands. It grows and grows, before you set it spinning. Balancing it on one finger, turn and send it into an orbit around you. Watch it circle. Pick up what appears to be an enormous sheet, throw it out in front of you. Let your arms undulate or ripple out to the sides to show it spreading. Stoop down and pick up a handful of dust, watching it slowly run out of your upraised hand.

But God comes like a shepherd.
He will feed his flock.
He will gather the little lambs in his arms,
and carry them in his bosom,
gently leading those that are with young.
He does not faint or grow weary,
His understanding is unsearchable.
He gives power to the faint,
and to him who has no might
He increases strength.

Turn away, and slowly turn back, now as The Shepherd, solemn, but not severe, with a long crook held in your hands. Plant it firmly to your side with your right hand. Open the gate to the sheepfold, and motion for the sheep to come out. Pick up one that is very small, and place in the folds of your 'garment' and walk forward. Put it down, and count the flock. Watch one sheep walking with a limp. Wrap a bandage around its foot and watch it gallop (sprint, run, gambol . . .) away. Don't be afraid to smile.

Even young men shall fall exhausted,
youths shall faint and grow weary.
But they who wait for the Lord
shall renew their strength:
They shall mount up with wings like eagles.
They shall run and not be weary.
They shall walk, and not faint.
Get you up to a high mountain.
Lift up your voice with strength and say,
Behold your God.

Begin walking with crook again but come to a sick/exhausted sheep and stop. Pick it up and tenderly but firmly hoist it over back of neck. Take up crook again and continue walking.

Freeze, turn and become slow-motion runner (*Chariots of Fire*) who sees and points ahead at majesty of God. Freeze and turn Us, turn back as The Shepherd again. Plant crook with one hand, and with sweeping hand gesture of welcome, love, acceptance, etc. to the audience.

The narration of this piece by Paul Burbridge, with music by Christopher Norton is available on the *Music for Mime* cassette mentioned on page 32.

26

The Heavenly City

(Words by Paul Burbridge, based on Hebrews 11.
Music for the original mime by Christopher Norton.)

Mime to narration, solo or group.
Approximate timing: four-to-seven minutes.

Outline

An opening mime sequence establishes a vigorous world of tangible things, people and experiences, such as relationships, eating and drinking, building, activity, exploring nature, getting wet, cooking, wind, laughter, tears, death, gravestones, rock, flowers, birth, writing, books games, etc. After a while the narration begins.

Narration

Eyes – colour, search, distance, change.
Hands – clutch, smooth, climb, put together.
Nose – breathe, perfume, discover, warning.
Mouth – bite, bitter, speak, kiss.
Ears – shout, attentive, whisper, respond.
Death – this little world, an ending.

Shape, texture, smell, language, sound, joy . . .
yet death, this little world, an ending.

Faith,
A window,
Death,
A door,
Beyond,
An invisible strength, the word of God, a better country,
not yet.

From the beginning, faith has been a window:

Abel offered worship,
God called him righteous.
He was brutally murdered;
his faith still speaks.

Enoch pleased God so much
God took him away.
His leaving was instant,
His faith has no grave.

Noah heeded God's warning;
Became heir to righteousness.
His household was saved;
His faith brings a rainbow.

Abram answered God's call
In pursuit of a promise.
Homeless and old,
His faith was rewarded.

Sarah believed God against nature.
He gave her a child

Whose life was protected
At the moment of death.
Her faith brought new life.

Moses fought for God's justice
He upheld the poor,
Delivered from death.
His faith freed a nation.

These all died in faith, staring through the open window, they saw what was to come. (Death a door, this little world, an ending.) By faith we cross the sea of death as if on dry land, a better country . . . not yet.

Faith is no escape from now.
It blazes in the teeth of torture, chains, violence, affliction.
It burns brightest in poverty, mockery, homelessness, abuse, decay. Faith conquers politics, enforces justice, receives promises, quenches the fires of evil, turns back destruction, silences false argument.
It is strength out of weakness,
Greater wealth than all the treasures of Egypt.

The reward is not yet.
We see it through the window of faith.
We enter through the door,
Convinced, assured, face to face with hope.
Those who die in faith, do not die – they wait to receive the promise:
God has prepared for them a city.

The citizens assemble, in succession, each incomplete without the next:
Abel, Enoch, Noah, Abraham, Sarah, Moses . . . (Fade out list of names at this point. If prerecording or using more

than one voice, carry on with list softly beneath the final section beginning 'Strangers and exiles'.) Rahab, Gideon, Lydia, John, Titus, Elizabeth, Hereward, Walter, Anne, Esther, Michael, Kevin, Thomas, Iran, Sharon, May, Charlotte, Peter . . .

Strangers and exiles in this little world
They look towards a better country,
having seen it and greeted it from afar.
God is not ashamed to be their God,
For he has prepared for them a city.
Whoever would draw near to God
Must look through the glass
And believe that God rewards those who seek him.
Life: this invisible world, a beginning.

For he has built them . . . a city.

27
Mime to Songs

This is a very appealing combination, and a good place to start work in public. The mime is freed from the responsibility of carrying all the meaning, while the song is enriched by the addition of visual activity. In some cases the lyrics strike home with the full force intended by the writer, simply because there is a character whom the listener can see and identify with.

There are two approaches: abstract, and character-centred.

In abstract, movements are strung together in a way that flows with the music, taking their force from the meaning provided by the words. It can become very dance-like, but it doesn't have to. It may be a series of mimed actions that embody or 'earth' what the lyrics are saying.

From storm-clouds to sunshine
You carry me high
You've given me wings
Now I'm learning to fly

from 'HEALING' by Maggie Dawn
copyright Thankyou Music 1986

This refrain could be accompanied by, for instance, a flying movement in which the arms become as powerful wings majestically propelling one (or appearing to) across the stage.

This is a good example of the kind of song you should look for. It must have one main theme, without getting too complicated about it, and two or three strong visual images that suggest a mime interpretation. And of course the music must grab you.

The other approach is character-centered. In this you create a simple story – it may be a day-in-the-life-of kind of sequence that counterpoints the lyrics of the song. The lyrics then become a commentary on the life, actions or mental state of the character. Or they could be God's thoughts about him, or his own inner thoughts.

Note that the mime does not necessarily connect with, or act out the lyrics, although it can be good if from time to time there occurs a poetic parallel or congruence. It may be subtle and ironic. For instance, the song might sing of the fire of God's love, just as the character is despondently lighting a cigarette and reflecting on his life which is empty of that love.

Or it may be very much more obvious, such as a repeated sequence of actions made by the character, indicating he doesn't know which way to walk, while the song is asking, do you know which way you're going, etc.

I am including a few suggestions for songs that in my opinion offer potential for mime interpretation, but the choice is up to you. Just remember, you are looking for something that not only appeals to you but also that will be appropriate for the context where you want to play it.

I should add that technically speaking any public performance or broadcasting (ie playing the tape) of a piece of music requires permission from the record company or the

PRS (Performing Rights Society) or both. But you can at least practice and entertain your family.

Below I offer a few suggestions (that are admittedly limited by my lack of musical knowledge).

1. *Noel Richards*, 'Broken Promises' from *The Danger Line* (Pioneer/Word).
   A good piece for two women, though it could be a man and a woman, especially if more pairs are brought in at the end.
2. *Maggie Dawn*, 'Healing' from *No Pretending* (Kingsway Records).
   Refrain quoted above. Probably solo mime, movement centred
   'All my Heart'. Also recorded by Wendy Craig – so two versions available.
3. *John Daniels*, 'Promises' from *Undivided Heart* (Kingsway Records).
   Possibly two person (male and female), character-centred, but mixed with abstract movement. You need to find a good sequence for the refrain.
   Also 'Inside His Heart'.
   Introspective and passionate. A song calling for brokenness. It needs a lot of depth in the acting.
4. *Martin Joseph*, 'Broken Wings Don't Always Heal to Fly' from *Treasure the Questions* (Pulse Records).
   A sensitive, heart-felt piece that requires equal sensitivity in the mime, along with enough confidence to know when to be still. There is pain in this song, and it should be underplayed in the mime, so avoid insensitive melodrama.

For a more up-beat piece the next song on the album, 'I Will Follow', could take a bold and passionate physical representation. Images that come to mind are: striding forward, (pressure walk), being blown down/off course, getting up and pressing on – adjusting course in order to follow, eyes fixed (on Jesus), etc.

Glossary

Technical Terms

Beat	The shortest unit of dramatic timing of a pause between two actions – practically speaking, usually just under a second.
Clic	A movement dynamic consisting of a tightening of the muscles before an action in order to show weight, and to give an indication of strength about to be expended (see Workshop 6).
fx	Effects, as in sound-effects.
Marche sur Place	A walk without changing place. It may be *en face* – facing the audience, or *profile* – sideways on to the audience.
Pause	A unit of dramatic timing. Longer than a beat, it can be any length as long as it's right.
Props	Properties. Items used by the actors on stage. Not so common in mime.
Toc	A movement dynamic which is at base a small explosion of energy. Often initiates or finishes a mime movement (see Workshop 2).

Wings	The sides of the stage out of the audience's view.

Abbreviations of Stage Directions

sL stage left	the left side of the stage, looking at the audience.
sR stage right	the right side of the stage, looking at the audience.
sC centre stage	
Us upstage	
UsC upstage centre	at the back of the stage, furthest from the audience, and central.
UsR upstage left	
UsR upstage right	
DsC downstage centre	
DsR downstage right	at the front of the stage, closest to the audience, and right.
DsL downstage left.	

APPENDIX 1

Mime Theatre

This is a performance style of mime that is marked by the use of imaginative and striking sound-effects made by the performers themselves. It is often a fast-moving almost cartoon style. There is a lot of energy, and a great sense of throwing it all out to the audience.

It was first popularised in Britain by a trio called 'The Moving Picture Mime Show'. The three met while training at the Jacques Lecoq Mime School in Paris, and subsequently developed a style that did a great deal to change the popular image of mime from the slightly ethereal, somewhat effeminate Marcel Marceau-type of white-face mime to a more robust, down-to-earth, very accessible and very eighties art form. They enjoyed great popularity with pieces such as 'The Seven Samurai', 'The Examination', 'The Lottery' and 'Handle with Care'. You might have seen their influence in the inventive, witty and energetic work of Pip and Rachel Hawthorn in their company 'Primary Colours'.

The lively knock-about feel of this style of mime is obviously more suited to street theatre and schools than church services. Don't think that makes it easy, however. It must still be mastered to be effective, like any other technical, artistic skill.

It must be controlled and tightly directed if it is not going to degenerate into a self-indulgent and incomprehensible rushing around the stage.

Perhaps the best parallel is an animated cartoon sequence, such as *Tom and Jerry* (or the whole of *Who Framed Roger Rabbit*?). Countless hours and great technical expertise go into producing a few minutes of fast moving comedy, and you can be sure there is no extraneous action in the final 'print' simply because somebody had a mediocre idea that nobody could be bothered to cut.

In fact you could do worse than studying a few old *Tom and Jerry* cartoons and imbibing the pace, the energy, the economy of movement and especially the comic timing.

Don't think such research frivolous. After all (if you need an excuse), you are trying to communicate in a culture where a whole generation and a half have been raised on cartoons.

Workshop 7, in particular, looks at the most notable aspect of this style of mime: the production of sound-effects by the performer.

When imitating a sound, there are two approaches.

One is similitude: making it as exactly as possible. Certain stand-up comedians are extremely good at this, using a microphone, and work their whole routines around it. Such virtuosity is entertaining but not really necessary for mime theatre.

The other is to go beyond the sound, to a commonly perceived aspect or dominant characteristic of that sound. It doesn't always matter that you can't vocalise perfectly, for instance, the exact electronic warbling note of a telephone, with all the harmonics and distortion. But you do have to achieve the rhythm – the timing – of it just right, if you want to please and convince.

Or take the swish of the automatic doors on an Intercity or

an underground train. There is a definite rhythm to the sound, and it is immensely pleasing to an audience when you get it spot-on.

Don't be put off by the difficulties, however. It is not always necessary to be that exact. Many times your aim is to advance the plot as quickly as possible. If the effect in question is *not* one that many people are going to identify with deeply, then it's not worth agonising over the minutest details.

So if you are trying to convey for example the experience of an Intercity 125 train, then you might want to show the automatic sliding doors. You could do this using your hands and arms to represent the edge sliding back. Your voice provides a 'whoosh' and 'hiss' while you move a straight, upright flat hand and forearm across in front of you, where the edge of the door is moving. The vital thing is to move it across with a rhythm, with punctuation, to match the sounds.

That is, of course, the other important consideration in this aspect of mime theatre: combining sound and action. Mechanical movement invariably produces sound. For example, there is the click or pair of clicks as a door handle is turned. When you imitate that, you do so within the mimed action of turning the imaginary handle.

The ascending squeal of a squeaky hinge, by contrast, often begins part-way through the movement of opening a door. It then ends with the door (as indicated by the hand, with arm fully extended) stopping in the arc it has described. The sound ceases exactly with the movement.

Some pointers on developing and practising sound-effects.

Listen to the world around you. Imitate as many sounds as you hear, in a given place. (Best practised alone, by and large, or you will get some funny looks.) Practise the Face Exercises in this book, followed by the Voice Exercises, concentrating on mouth, lips and tongue. Make a study of voice and sound production, head, throat and chest tones, breath control and breathing from the diaphragm, etc. (See Cicely Berry, *Voice and The Actor*).

Finally, expand your imagination. Try making sounds of animals, machines, activities. Go further: colours, shapes, the creation.

Appendix 2

Mime in Public and Private Worship

Public

The successful integration of a mime piece into a service of worship depends so much on the character of the worship and on the style of the performer that it is not possible to lay down hard-and-fast rules. Nevertheless there is great potential for sensitive and moving contributions to the ministry of teaching and preaching. Mime has a unique potential among the arts in church because of the way it engages the imagination within a narrative: it tells a story, reveals a character, and gives pictures for interpretation. (Read *Steps of Faith*, Chapter 2 on the justifications for its use.)

Here are some of the forms mime can take in worship.

(1) The Short Sketch.

A self-contained piece of drama that can illustrate a point, or open up a subject or topic, such as unemployment or marital disharmony. One particularly good method is to add a series of brief vignettes to a sermon – each lasting no longer than a minute – to flesh out the talk. This requires working closely with the preacher. The preacher can set the scene of the mime, and take up the point being made, so the mime does not have to try and say it all. It does not even have to be a complete drama. An example: two or three short pieces between two characters to show how bitterness and aggression escalates from very small incidents, where there is no trust.

(2) Mime to a Bible Reading.

This can make well-known verses fresh, and bring the meaning alive. It can be a simple series of gestures, postures or mimed actions to interpret the reading in movement. Or it can be done to a script of arranged Scripture verses, such as 'Behold Your God' (Isaiah 40) and 'The Heavenly City' (Hebrew 11) in this book and 'Valley of the Bones' (Ezekiel 37) in *Steps of Faith*. See also 'Wisdom and Folly' (from Proverbs) and 'The Light of the World' (John's gospel) in *Time to Act* by Paul Burbridge and Murray Watts (Hodder and Stoughton, 1979).

(3) A Modern-day parable.

The parables that Jesus used in his teaching were simple stories memorably told, conveying a profound spiritual truth. There are a variety of reasons why the Lord taught in this way. He himself spoke of hiding the truth from those who were not seeking (Matt. 13:13–15). The ease with which such a form is preserved and handed down in an oral tradition is another reason. Perhaps, too, parables crystallise truth in a poetic way. Thus they can often cut to the point more clearly than a doctrinal formulation while at the same time avoiding rigidity and legalism, which is death to life in the Spirit.

Of course I would not claim all of that for the couple of modern-day parables in this book, but they do have a point to make. See 'The Chocolate Box' (p. 112) and 'The Good News is Like . . . ' (p. 130). See also 'The Widow's Mites', in *Time to Act*.

Mime used in prophetic pictures

This is what you might call the experimental end of the spectrum, and is obviously not appropriate for many church situations. Therefore I will only put forward a few ideas in outline.

But first, a word of encouragement – and a word of warning. Remember Paul's directive in 1 Cor. 4: – 'Eagerly desire the spiritual gifts, especially the gift of prophecy,' and in verse 5, 'I would rather have you prophesy' (not forgetting of course, the need for love to crown all the gifts).

The warning is from the Old Testament, and it is the third commandment: 'You shall not misuse the name of the Lord your God'. Commonly thought to be directed against blasphemy, this can also be a prohibition against false prophets, in that they are not to claim the authority of God for what they say. Roger Forster observes. 'The spirit of prophecy is the spirit of Jesus. It will reveal Jesus in some way to me.'

I do not intend to explore prophecy here as there is excellent teaching available from people such as Roger Forster. Rather, I want to suggest that in the context of informal worship in the family of God, where spiritual gifts are being exercised, there may be a place for prophetic pictures that are acted out as well as spoken.

Such a picture will usually be followed by a spoken interpretation – you don't want the congregation to have to puzzle out an imperfect mine in order to understand what God may be saying!

The way the picture is handled will vary according to the style of leadership, but a mime picture, like a spoken prophesy, will normally be cleared with a leader before being presented to the congregation. It may be a picture that the individual who is presenting it has had, or it may have been given to him or her for acting out by someone else who has a prophetic gift but not an acting gift.

It is not the case that 'anything goes, as long as you're sincere.' Great sensitivity is required (as well as considerable boldness!). Such experimental worship should also take place within a non-threatening atmosphere where firm but gentle leadership instils confidence, and the spirit of love banishes fear of criticism. A tall order I know.

I said this was experimental, but in fact what I am suggesting goes back to Jeremiah and Ezekiel, who often mimed their prophecies to God's people. Mimed prophecy can be a mime picture with a spoken interpretation, or it can be an acted-out symbol, parable or illustration.

For example:

1. A dirty robe or coat is removed and replaced with a clean one.
2. A cup is filled from 'heaven' and enjoyed, but then not shared and so not filled again.
3. A door will not budge – until the key is found.
4. An unprimed, squeaky pump gives no water, until a cup of water primes it – then the rainstorm which surpasses it.
5. A wall is built around you – until you can't get out.

Use your imagination to see whether these could have a spiritual interpretation. However, they are mentioned here for practice, so to speak. In church worship God gives particular pictures for a particular time, place and people.

Three pieces of advice:

1. Remember that prophecy is not *fore*telling (the future), it is *forth*-telling (God's word).

2. Prophecy is for the edification of believers and the building up of the body of Christ.
3. Ask for the Holy Spirit. Seek anointing – not fanciful, blessed thoughts. God must give the *what*, the *how*, and the *when* – otherwise it has no meaning.

Still interested? Try Workshop 9 to experiment with the imaginative process that goes into the exercise of this gift.

Mime in private devotion

'Mime in front of God? I'd feel awfully silly.'
In that case I suggest you read my wife's half of *Steps of Faith*, on dance in worship. See also *Moving Prayer* by Rosemary Budd (MARC Europe, 1987).

There are two areas – worship and intercession.

Examples of mime in private worship are:

1. Opening arms out to show vulnerability, perhaps to a song like 'Jesus, take me as I am.'
2. Kneeling in submission.
3. Prostrate in awe and self-abasement.
4. Hands clenched, holding the day's worries and tension – then turning them up, opening them and releasing those worries to God.
5. Leaping for joy.

Examples of mime in intercession are:

1. Arms comforting, walking with a person who is not there and for whom you are praying. Hug them as you would want God to hug them and surround them with his love.

2. Hands opening, as a flower, representing a life opening to God.
3. Palms lifting up a person or situation to God's 'notice'.
4. Wield a sword to cut off Satan's influence.
5. Push back the darkness from a situation or individual.
6. Stretch out hands to receive or to give forgiveness.

Many other things are possible. It is an area for personal discovery and you should experiment in the way that you are most comfortable. Try to see it as *inking in* your prayer, demonstrating your commitment, (overcome your embarrassment, for him!) and letting the Spirit move you. You won't know till you try!

Bibliography

Barker, Clive. *Theatre Games*. (Methuen: London, 1977).

Beall, Patricia & Barker, Martha K. *The Folk Arts in Renewal*. (Hodder & Stoughton: London, 1980).

Brandes, Donna & Phillips, Howard. *Gamesters' Handbook*. (Hutchinson: London, 1977).

Burbridge, Paul & Watts, Murray. *Time to Act*. (Hodder & Stoughton: London, 1979).

Darius, Adam. *The Adam Darius Method*. (Latonia Publishers: London, 1984).

Felner, Mira. *Apostles of Silence – The Modern French Mimes*. (Associated University Presses: London, 1985).

Loeschke, Maravene S. *All about Mime*. (Prentice-Hall: New Jersey, 1982).

Miles-Brown, John. *Acting: A Drama Studio Source Book*. (Peter Owen: London, 1985).

Nobleman, Roberta. *Mime and Masks*. (New Plays Books: Rowayton, Conn. 1979).

Pecknold, Adrian. *Mime: The Step Beyond Words*. (New Canada Publications: Toronto, 1982).

Scher, Anna & Verrall, Charles. *100+ Ideas for Drama*. (Heinemann: London, 1975).

Shepard, Richmond. *Mime: The Technique of Silence*. (Drama Book Specialists: New York, 1971).

Stevenson, Geoffrey & Judith. *Steps of Faith*. (Kingsway Publications: Eastbourne, 1984).
Stolzenberg, Mark. *Exploring Mime*. (Oak Tree Press: Cowdon, 1979).
Toomey, Susie K. *Mime Ministry*. (Meriwether Publishing Ltd: Colorado Springs, 1986).

One Stage Further

by Nigel Forde

In the tradition of Riding Lights Theatre Company's usual wit and polish, *One Stage Further* provides more entertaining and fast-moving sketches for performance by church groups and other amateur companies. Here Nigel Forde has written sixteen sketches and one full-length play, *Angel at Large,* to make us laugh, to make us think, and to make us want to change.

Doctor: It sounds as if you'd have done better to go to your dentist rather than come to me.
Rector: To a dentist?
Doctor: I think so, yes. I think what you've got there is a hollow truth. (Peers) Just as I thought. There's a large truth here with a great gaping hole in it. Too many sugary choruses…

'A collection of sketches on spiritual and moral themes that leap off the page with verve and wit.'

James Fox in his *Preface*

MARC
Monarch Publications

Laughter In Heaven

Edited by Murray Watts

Fifteen superb sketches and a modern morality play from the Riding Lights Theatre Company.

The five contributors to this book share faith in Christ and a love of laughter. Both are infectious as the audience is drawn in to the drama, the fun and the inspiration.

'A valuable addition to the drama bookshelf.'
Church of England Newspaper

'A good deal of bite.'
Guardian

MURRAY WATTS has established a reputation for innovative, fast-moving, and professional drama. Those who read and perform these Riding Lights sketches will not be disappointed.

MARC
Monarch Publications

The Greatest Burger Ever Sold

by Nick McIvor

'Jesus, son of Joseph, was born into a working-class family in the provincial town of Nazareth.' So begins the story of the best-known character in history, and yet there are still a host of unanswered questions about his life and work. How was he treated by the press? Where did the disciples go to school? Did his miracles affect health-insurance premiums? *The Greatest Burger Ever Sold* confronts these issues.

The sketches here have appeared at universities and festivals around the country including Mayfest (Glasgow), Greenbelt (Northampton) and York. Described by *The Scotsman* at the 1983 Edinburgh Fringe as 'imaginative', 'brutal', and 'acutely observed', they relate the life of Christ through a series of eye-witnesses who were clearly implied, if not explicitly mentioned in the biblical accounts.

Would Jesus have attracted commercial sponsorship? What did Joseph's mother think? Find out in: *The Greatest Burger Ever Sold.*

NICK McIVOR is an actor, comedian and scriptwriter for stage and television. He lives in London.

Minstrel
Monarch Publications